Poetry
Comprehension Skills

Contents

Grade 4
Poetry Comprehension Skills

Introduction

This book is designed to help students become better readers through the reading of poetry. The IRA/NCTE Standards for the English Language Arts list as the first recommendation: "Students read a wide range of print and nonprint texts to build an understanding of texts, of themselves, and of the cultures of the United States and the world…." Poetry is a form of literature easily read and enjoyed by students of all ages. Children's books often use the rhythm and rhyme of poetry to engage young readers. Poetry helps develop language skills and is often used in phonemic awareness techniques. Moreover, since poetry often uses figurative speech, it encourages imagination and creative thinking. As students progress, their enjoyment of poetry grows to encompass different forms and styles. Most students not only enjoy reading poetry, but they enjoy creating their own verse as well. Finally, most assessment tests now include poetry. These tests include both multiple choice and short-answer questions. It is important that students become comfortable with the format so as to be confident when they encounter it in testing situations.

The Poetry Series

This reproducible poetry series will supplement any reading program. Each lesson tests comprehension skills as well as offers suggestions for vocabulary and fluency development, two essential skills for reading and language development.

Organization of the Poetry Series

The book is divided into four thematic units which will help the teacher integrate poetry into other content areas. The units are On the Silly Side; People, Young and Old; Naturally Nature; and Moving On. There are five poems in each unit. The lesson components are explained below.

Teacher Information

The first page of every lesson provides explicit instructions for teaching the poem. There are specific sections that address multiple skills. To begin, each poem is summarized. A list of words that children may find difficult to read or understand is included as well. Another section lists a specific poetry standard and outlines an activity that will help students explore the concept. A third section outlines how to introduce the poem and the vocabulary words, as well as includes ideas for fluency practice. Finally, a fun and creative writing suggestion helps children think about the topic or a specific skill to extend the lesson.

Poem

The poems were selected to complement topics taught at each grade level. Illustrations on the page support the topic to help children better understand the content.

Assessment

Each poem is followed by a seven-question assessment. The first six questions are in a standardized-test format and focus on six important comprehension skills. They always follow a prescribed order:

1. Facts The first question focuses on literal comprehension. Students identify pieces of factual information. They look for details that tell who, what, when, where, and how.

2. Sequence The second question refers to sequence. Students practice identifying the order of events or the steps in a process.

3. Context In the third question, students are required to practice using all the words in the poem to understand unfamiliar words. Students become aware of the relationships between words, phrases, and sentences.

4. Main Idea In this question, students will identify the overall point made in the poem. Students must be able to differentiate between the main idea and details.

5. Conclusion The fifth question requires students to draw conclusions. Conclusions are not stated in the reading but must be formulated. Students draw conclusions based only on the information in the poem.

6. Inference The sixth question asks students to make inferences by combining their own knowledge and experience with what they read. They put the facts together to make a reasonable inference about something that is not stated in the poem.

7. Short Answer The final question requires that children write a brief response to a higher-level question.

Other Components

• **Standards** A list of grade-level, poetry-specific standards is found on page 5. A chart highlights in which lesson each standard is introduced.

• **Glossary** Poetry terms and definitions for use by the teacher and older students are given on page 6. Some of the elements are not introduced to younger students in this poetry series since they require advanced knowledge.

• **General Assessment** A two-page assessment is found on pages 7 and 8. It can be used as a pretest to gauge students' understanding of the comprehension skills. It can also be used as a posttest to determine improvements after exposure to poetic literature.

• **Graphic Organizers** Five graphic organizers are provided on pages 9–13 to support different activities and skill development suggested in various lessons.

Poetry Standards • Grade 4

The following standards focus specifically on poetry and are accepted by many states as important to students in the fourth grade.

Standard	Lesson
Distinguish between fiction, nonfiction, poetry, plays, and narratives	1, 8, 11, 20
Identify a concrete poem	14
Identify a haiku	16
Identify a limerick	5
Identify words that develop auditory skills, including alliteration, onomatopoeia, assonance, and consonance	4
Identify rhyme	6, 10, 13, 17
Identify rhythm	2
Recognize the use of repetition	9
Recognize the use of similes, metaphors, and personification	3, 7, 12, 15, 18, 19
Describe characters, setting, and important events in fiction and poetry	All poems
Read stories, poems, and passages with fluency and expression	All poems

Resources: Standards
Poetry: Grade 4, SV 9894-9

Glossary

alliteration the repetition of the same beginning sound, usually a consonant, in a phrase or line of poetry. Tongue twisters use alliteration. Example: *She sells seashells by the seashore.*

analogy a likeness between two things that are not alike in other ways. Example: *the wings of a bird and the arms of a person*

assonance the repetition of similar vowel sounds in words so they are close in sound, but do not rhyme. Example: *She feeds the deer.*

ballad a long poem written about a famous person or event

cinquain a formula poem that has five lines and a total of 22 syllables, distributed in a specific 2–4–6–8–2 pattern

concrete a poem in which the words, letters, or shape of the poem match the topic

consonance the close repetition of identical consonant sounds before and after different vowels. Example: *flip—flop; feel—fill*

diamante a formula poem that is shaped like a diamond, and the words describe opposite ideas

haiku a formula poem that has three lines and a total of 17 syllables, often distributed in a specific 5–7–5 pattern

imagery the author's use of description and words to create pictures in the reader's mind

limerick a humorous formula poem that has five lines, an "aabba" rhyming pattern, and a specific rhythm

metaphor the comparison of two things in which one is said to be another. Metaphors do not use the words *like* or *as*. Example: *The lake was a golden mirror.*

meter the cadence, or beat, of a poem

onomatopoeia a sound device in which a word makes the sound. Examples: *crash, bang*

personification a device in which human qualities and ideas are given to things. Example: *The wind whispered through the trees.*

poetry an expression of ideas or feeling in words. Poetry usually has form, rhythm, and rhyme.

repetition a sound device in which sounds, words, or phrases are repeated to emphasize a point

rhyme two or more lines that end with rhyming words

rhyming words words that end in the same sounds

rhythm the repeated meter, or beat, in a poem

simile the comparison of two things that are not really alike by using the words *like* or *as*. Example: *Her smile was like sunshine.*

sonnet a poem with 14 lines and a specific rhyming and rhythm pattern

stanza a group of related lines in a poem

tanka a formula poem that has five lines and a total of 31 syllables, distributed in a specific 5–7–5–7–7 pattern

Nest Eggs
by Robert Louis Stevenson

Birds all the summer day
   Flutter and quarrel
Here in the arbor-like
   Tent of the laurel.

Here in the fork
   The brown nest is seated;
For little blue eggs
   The mother keeps heated.

While we stand watching her
   Staring like gabies,
Safe in each egg are the
   Bird's little babies.

Soon the frail eggs they shall
   Chip, and upspringing
Make all the April woods
   Merry with singing.

Younger than we are,
   O children, and frailer,
Soon in the blue air they'll be,
   Singer and sailor.

We, so much older,
   Taller and stronger,
We shall look down on the
   Birdies no longer.

They shall go flying
   With musical speeches
High overhead in the
   Tops of the beeches.

In spite of our wisdom
   And sensible talking,
We on our feet must go
   Plodding and walking.

Go on to the next page.

Assessment
Poetry: Grade 4, SV 9894-9

Understand the Poem

Nest Egg: Assessment

🖋 **Think about the poem. Then answer the questions. Fill in the circle next to the correct answer.**

1. This poem talks about which month?
- Ⓐ June
- Ⓑ August
- Ⓒ May
- Ⓓ April

2. Before the baby birds hatch,
- Ⓐ they learn to fly.
- Ⓑ they are in blue eggs.
- Ⓒ they sing.
- Ⓓ they walk.

3. The eggs are frail. "Frail" means
- Ⓐ easily broken.
- Ⓑ light blue.
- Ⓒ very young.
- Ⓓ nearly broken.

4. The poem tells about how
- Ⓐ birds feed their babies.
- Ⓑ even young birds fly high above people.
- Ⓒ birds do not get along.
- Ⓓ birds do not care for their babies.

5. The birds in the poem were hatched
- Ⓐ in the summer.
- Ⓑ in the fall.
- Ⓒ in the spring.
- Ⓓ in the winter.

6. The poet probably
- Ⓐ thinks that birds are happier than people are.
- Ⓑ would like to be able to fly like a bird.
- Ⓒ lives in the woods.
- Ⓓ sings like a bird.

7. How do you know that "Nest Eggs" is a poem?

_____

_____

Assessment
Poetry: Grade 4, SV 9894-9

Word Card

What Is the Word?
Write the word here.

_____

What Does the Word Mean?
Write the meaning here.

_____
_____
_____
_____
_____
_____
_____

What Does the Word Stand For?
Draw a picture of it here.

How Can You Use the Word?
Write a sentence using the word here.

_____
_____
_____
_____
_____
_____
_____

Resources: Word Card
Poetry: Grade 4, SV 9894-9

Word Wheel

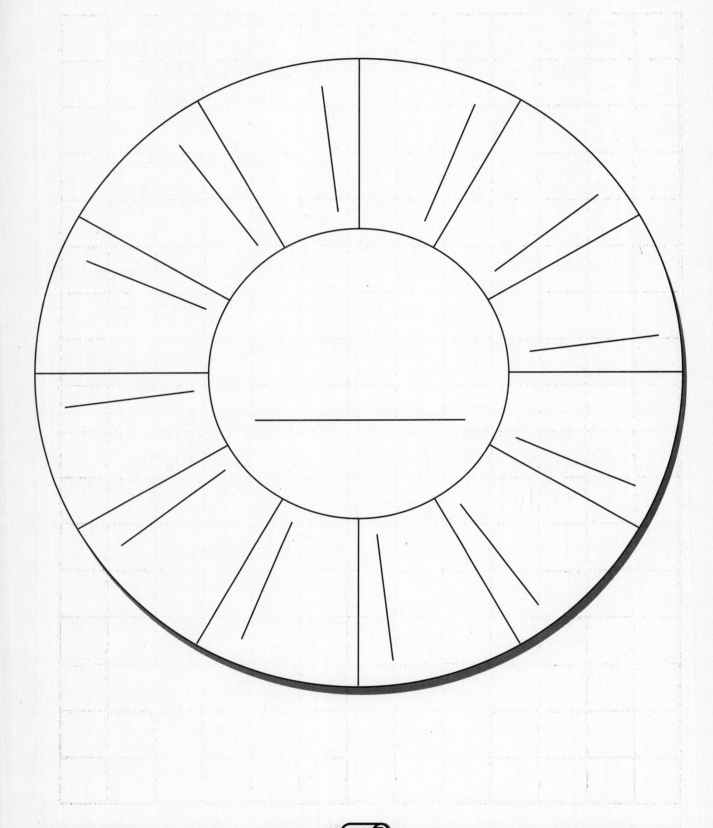

Resources: Word Wheel
Poetry: Grade 4, SV 9894-9

Graph

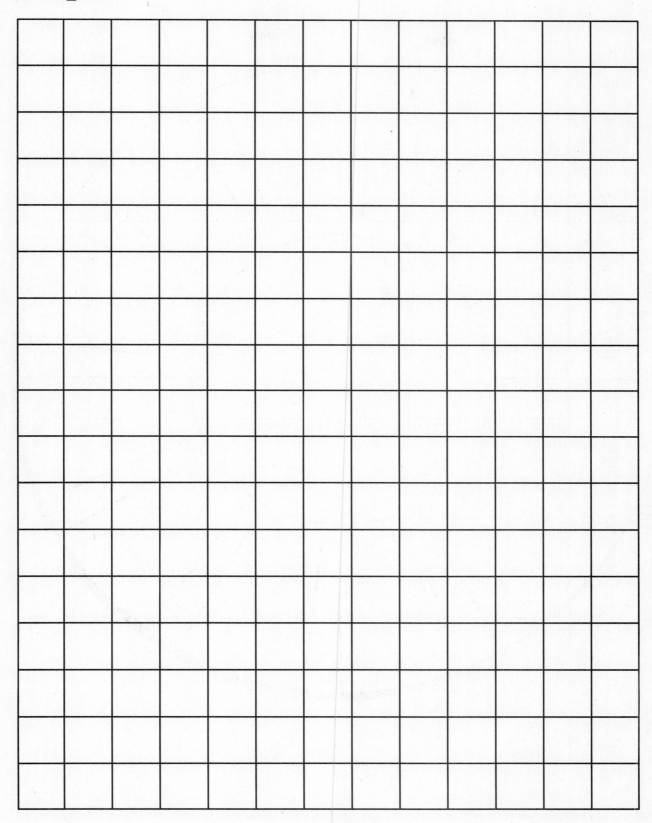

Resources: Graph

Poetry: Grade 4, SV 9894-9

KWHL Chart

K (What Do I KNOW?)	W (Want do I WANT to Know?)	H (HOW will I learn?)	L (What did I LEARN?)

Resources: KWHL Chart
Poetry: Grade 4, SV 9894-9

Venn Diagram

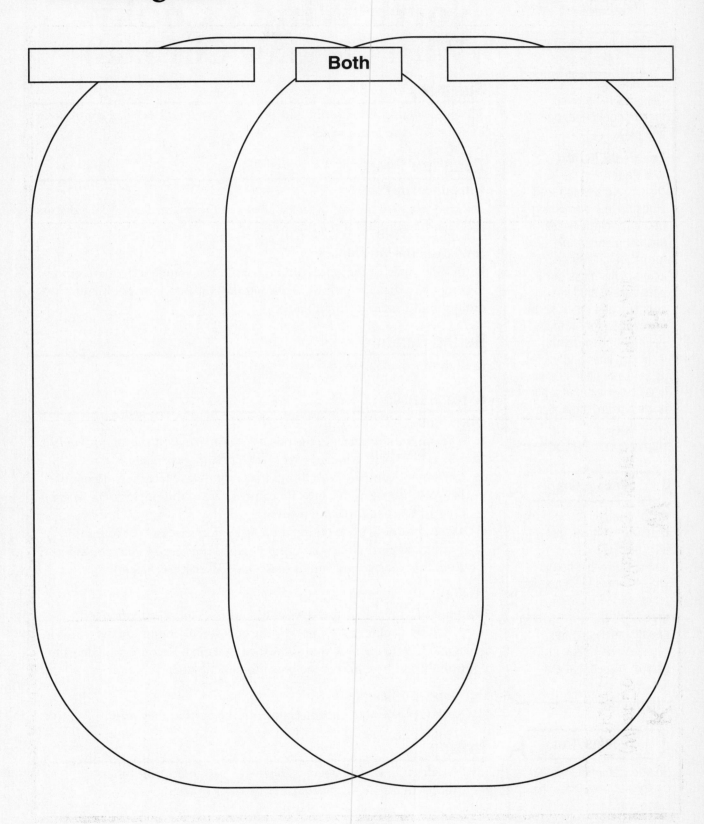

Both

The Moon's the North Wind's Cooky
(What the Little Girl Said)

Poetry Skill: Format

Standard
Distinguish between fiction, nonfiction, poetry, and plays

Explore the Format of a Poem
Display a story and lead students in a discussion of the format they see, including paragraph formation and sentence length. Then pass out the poem. Have students compare and contrast the poem and story formats. Point out poem terms, including lines and verses, as students identify them. Finally, explain that a poem is a snapshot of an idea or feeling.

Vocabulary

crisp–crunchy
crumble–to break into little pieces
den–a room in a house where people talk and play together
greedy–wanting everything
kneads–mixes dough
rim–the outer edge
scraps–pieces that are left over

Teacher Tips

Point out to students that *cooky* and *cookie* are the same word.

Summary

The poet whimsically describes the phases of the moon as being controlled by the north and south winds.

Read the Poem

Introduce the Poem
Ask students to draw four different phases of the moon. Then briefly discuss the scientific reasons for the changes.

Introduce the Vocabulary
Distribute copies of the word card on page 9. Have students work in groups to complete a card for each word. Gather the students and ask different groups to discuss a word you name.

During Reading

Read the poem aloud to students.

After Reading

Questions
1. Who are the characters in the poem? (*North Wind, Moon, South Wind*)
2. Why is the North Wind greedy? (*He keeps eating the moon.*)
3. A metaphor compares two things that are unlike. Metaphors do not use the words *like* or *as.* What two metaphors are in this poem? (*The Moon is a cookie. The South Wind is a baker.*)
4. Personification is giving things human characteristics. What are some examples of personification in this poem? (*The North Wind bites the cookie. The South wind kneads clouds and bakes a new moon.*)

Fluency
Point out that an author uses special text features to call attention to important parts of text. Discuss why the poet might emphasize the words in italics and how to read them to show their meaning. Encourage students to rehearse the last two lines of the poem to develop fluency.

Develop Oral Language
Have partners reread the poem, acting out the parts as they read.

Writing

Invite students to write a poem using metaphors to describe other occurrences in nature, such as seasons or kinds of weather.

The Moon's the North Wind's Cooky
(What the Little Girl Said)
by Vachel Lindsay

The Moon's the North Wind's cooky,
He bites it day by day,
Until there's but a rim of scraps
That crumble all away.

The South Wind is the baker,
He kneads clouds in his den,
And bakes a crisp new Moon that…*greedy
North…Wind…eats…again!*

Name _____   Date _____

Understand the Poem

The Moon's the North Wind's Cooky (What the Little Girl Said): Assessment

Think about the poem. Then answer the questions. Fill in the circle next to the correct answer.

1. Who eats the Moon?
   Ⓐ the North Wind
   Ⓑ the South Wind
   Ⓒ the baker
   Ⓓ the clouds

2. After the South Wind bakes a new Moon,
   Ⓐ he eats it.
   Ⓑ the clouds decorate it.
   Ⓒ the Moon is happy.
   Ⓓ the North Wind eats it.

3. The word "kneads" means
   Ⓐ must have.
   Ⓑ mixes dough.
   Ⓒ parts of the legs that bend.
   Ⓓ blows.

4. The poem is mostly about
   Ⓐ baking cookies.
   Ⓑ windy times of the year.
   Ⓒ the changes in the moon.
   Ⓓ eating food.

5. The poet compares the Moon to a cookie because
   Ⓐ the moon looks like a cookie as it is being eaten.
   Ⓑ they both are round and crisp.
   Ⓒ bakers make both of them.
   Ⓓ they both change shape each month.

6. You can see a new moon
   Ⓐ at the beginning of the month.
   Ⓑ at the end of the year.
   Ⓒ when the North Wind bakes it.
   Ⓓ each night.

7. How do you know that this is a poem?

_____

_____

www.harcourtschoolsupply.com
© Harcourt Achieve Inc. All rights reserved.

16

Lesson 1 • The Moon's the North Wind's Cooky: Poem Assessment
Poetry: Grade 4, SV 9894-9

Name _____   Date _____

Homophones

Some words sound alike, but they have different spellings and meanings.

   Example: I **ate eight** nuts.

   ate = chewed and swallowed food

   eight = the number 8

Read each sentence. Circle the words that sound alike. Then find the words in a dictionary. Write the meaning of each word.

1. The baker needs to add more flour when he kneads the bread dough.

   _____

   _____

2. They knew when the new moon would begin.

   _____

   _____

3. There's the car that is theirs.

   _____

   _____

4. Grandmother went by the bakery to buy cookies.

   _____

   _____

[from] The Blind Men and the Elephant

Summary

Six different men touch an elephant in different places and describe the animal in different ways.

Read the Poem

Introduce the Poem

In advance, cut up a whole pineapple so that the top, outer rind, fruit, and hard inner core are separated. Put each in a container so that they are not visible. Tell students that the parts that are in the containers belong to the same thing. Then invite four volunteers to feel the different parts while blindfolded and describe what they are feeling. Write their descriptions down and challenge the class to identify what the mystery item is. Reveal the pineapple after studying the poem in the After Reading section.

Introduce the Vocabulary

Write the vocabulary words and the definitions on the board. Lead students in a brief discussion of the words. Then have students create a word puzzle with the words using the graph on page 11. Challenge students to write sentences as clues to complete the puzzle.

During Reading

Invite volunteers to read the poem.

After Reading

Questions

1. Why did the second man think the elephant was like a spear? (*He felt the sharp tusk.*)
2. Do you think the men are wise? Why or why not? (*Most likely answer: The men are not wise because they are not listening to each other. Each thinks that he is right.*)
3. (Return to the introduction activity. Display the different pineapple parts.) How was the experience of feeling the pineapple like the experience of the characters in the poem? (*Answers will vary.*)
4. What can you learn from the poem and the pineapple experience? (*Answers will vary.*)

Fluency

Point out words that students might find difficult because of the time period. Write them on the board and discuss their meanings. Have them rehearse the words for automaticity. Then encourage groups of students to assign parts and read the verses.

Poetry Skill: Rhythm

Standard
Identify rhythm

Explore Meter
Explain to students that many poems have a specific rhythm, or beat. The beat is called *meter*. Write the first two lines on the board and draw lines to divide the syllables: It/was/six/men/of/In/do/stan/To/learn/ing/much/in/clined. Then write the number of syllables at the end of both lines. Then assign groups and verses. Have them find the number of syllables for the assigned verse and compare results.

Vocabulary

bawl–to cry loudly
deny–to say that something is not true
disputed–argued
eager–wanting very much to do something
grope–to feel with the hands
inclined–wanting to do something
marvel–something amazing
observation–the act of noticing
opinion–what you think about something
resembles–is like

[from] The Blind Men and the Elephant

by Godfrey Saxe

It was six men of Indostan
To learning much inclined,
Who went to see the elephant
(Though all of them were blind),
That each by observation
Might satisfy his mind.

The *First* approached the Elephant,
And happening to fall
Against his broad and sturdy side,
At once began to bawl:
"God bless me! but the Elephant
Is very like a wall!"

The *Second,* feeling of the tusk,
Cried, "Ho! what have we here,
So very round and smooth and sharp?
To me 'tis mighty clear—
This wonder of an Elephant
Is very like a spear!"

The *Third* approached the animal,
And happening to take
The squirming trunk within his hands,
Thus boldly up and spake:
"I see," quoth he, "the Elephant
Is very like a snake!"

The *Fourth* reached out an eager hand,
And felt about the knee.
"What most this wondrous beast is like
Is mighty plain," quoth he;
"'Tis clear enough the Elephant
Is very like a tree!"

The *Fifth,* who chanced to touch the ear,
Said: "Even the blindest man
Can tell what this resembles most;
Deny the fact who can,
This marvel of an Elephant
Is very like a fan!"

The *Sixth* no sooner had begun
About the beast to grope,
Than, seizing on the swinging tail
That fell within his scope,
"I see," quoth he, "the Elephant
Is very like a rope!"

And so these men of Indostan
Disputed loud and long,
Each in his own opinion
Exceeding stiff and strong,
Though each was partly in the right,
And all were in the wrong!

Name _____   Date _____

[from] The Blind Men and the Elephant: Assessment

Think about the poem. Then answer the questions. Fill in the circle next to the correct answer.

1. The six men in the poem are
   - Ⓐ deaf.
   - Ⓑ young.
   - Ⓒ blind.
   - Ⓓ happy.

2. The third man who touches the elephant thinks
   - Ⓐ that the elephant is like a tree.
   - Ⓑ that the elephant is like a snake.
   - Ⓒ that the elephant is like a fan.
   - Ⓓ that the elephant is like a rope.

3. The six men disputed about what they had touched. "Disputed" means
   - Ⓐ discussed.
   - Ⓑ agreed.
   - Ⓒ argued.
   - Ⓓ laughed.

4. The main idea of this poem is that
   - Ⓐ blind men cannot know what is right.
   - Ⓑ a tiny bit of information about something is not enough to make a decision about it.
   - Ⓒ it takes only a short time to be an expert about something.
   - Ⓓ smart people are always right.

5. You can tell that the six men
   - Ⓐ think they are very wise.
   - Ⓑ know a lot about elephants.
   - Ⓒ do not know each other well.
   - Ⓓ listen carefully to others.

6. Which word would best describe the six men?
   - Ⓐ brilliant
   - Ⓑ sloppy
   - Ⓒ foolish
   - Ⓓ polite

7. What can you learn from the poem "The Blind Men and the Elephant"?

_____

_____

Name _____   Date _____

Synonyms

A synonym is a word that means the same or almost the same as another word.

    Examples: start—begin   happy—glad

Read each sentence. Find a word in the box that means the same or almost the same as the word or words in dark print. Write the word on the line.

approached inclined	bawl resembles	disputed sturdy	grope squirming

1. Maria saw something **wiggling** in the bushes.

    _____

2. She began to **cry loudly** for help.

    _____

3. Her friend, Leo, **came near**.

    _____

4. "It **looks like** a snake," Maria said.

    _____

5. Leo used a **strong** tree branch to check the bushes.

    _____

6. He did not want to **feel** in the leaves with his hands.

    _____

7. Leo did not find anything and was **wanting** to believe that Maria had been seeing things.

    _____

8. The friends **argued** for several minutes before deciding they should forget the event.

    _____

How to Eat a Poem

Poetry Skill: Metaphor

Standard
Recognize the use of similes, metaphors, and personification

Explore Metaphors
Explain to students that a metaphor is a poetic device in which two things that are unlike are compared so that one is said to be another. Metaphors do not use the words *like* or *as*. Then discuss the examples, *The green grass was a carpet under our feet*, and *The room was an oven.* Challenge students to identify the metaphor in the poem.

Vocabulary

juice–the liquid from fruit
napkin–paper or cloth used to wipe your lips or fingers
polite–acting with manners
rind–the tough outer covering of a fruit
ripe–fully grown and ready to eat
pit–the seed of fruit

Summary

Eve Merriam, a contemporary poet, encourages readers to enjoy poetry by taking a big, juicy bite of one.

Read the Poem

Introduce the Poem
Invite students to draw a picture of their favorite food. Then have them form small groups and talk about why they like the food and special things they do as they eat it. Then ask students to review the vocabulary words to predict what food the poem might talk about.

Introduce the Vocabulary
Use the graph on page 11 to make a word find puzzle, writing the words students are to find below the puzzle. Duplicate the activity page for students. Have partners circle the words in the puzzle and find the words in a dictionary. Ask them to write a sentence using each word.

During Reading

Invite a volunteer to read the poem.

After Reading

Activity
Remind students that a metaphor compares two unlike things. Then ask them what two things the poet compares in "How to Eat a Poem." Challenge partners to complete a Venn diagram from page 13 to show the similarities and differences that the poet says exist as well as ones students can identify.

Fluency
Lead students in a discussion of the mood of the poem. Ask if the poet is excited or calm, or if she is happy or sad. Then read the poem in several ways: fast and excited, slow and melancholy, and calm and happy. Have students tell which speed and voice reflect the mood of the poem. Point out how the words and images dictate the mood. Finally, have students practice reading the poem expressively.

Develop Oral Language
Have partners reread the poem out loud and then explain in their own words the meaning of the poem.

Writing

Remind students that they drew a picture of a favorite food. Ask them to compare the food to something else. Then challenge them to use "How to Eat a Poem" as a format guide for writing a metaphor poem of their own.

How to Eat a Poem
by Eve Merriam

Don't be polite.
Bite in.
Pick it up with your fingers and lick the juice that
    may run down your chin.
It is ready and ripe now, whenever you are.

You do not need a knife or fork or spoon
or plate or napkin or tablecloth.

For there is no core
or stem
or rind
or pit
or seed
or skin
to throw away.

Understand the Poem

How to Eat a Poem: Assessment

Think about the poem. Then answer the questions. Fill in the circle next to the correct answer.

1. What does the poet tell the reader to do with a poem?
   Ⓐ Read it.
   Ⓑ Bite in.
   Ⓒ Skin it.
   Ⓓ Throw it away.

2. What does the poet say to do after picking up the poem?
   Ⓐ Lick the juice.
   Ⓑ Remove the seeds.
   Ⓒ Taste it.
   Ⓓ Cut it with a knife.

3. Which words from the poem have the same meaning?
   Ⓐ skin, rind
   Ⓑ ripe, core
   Ⓒ polite, bite
   Ⓓ rind, pit

4. The poem is called "How to Eat a Poem" because
   Ⓐ the poet does not like manners.
   Ⓑ the poet believes poetry should be read with enthusiasm.
   Ⓒ the poet enjoys fruit.
   Ⓓ it is less messy than eating fruit.

5. Which of the following is NOT a fruit that the poem could be compared to?
   Ⓐ a pineapple
   Ⓑ an orange
   Ⓒ a watermelon
   Ⓓ a banana

6. Why did the poet write "How to Eat a Poem"?
   Ⓐ to teach readers about food
   Ⓑ to tell step-by-step the correct way to read a poem
   Ⓒ to tell readers a funny story
   Ⓓ to persuade readers to enjoy poetry the way they enjoy fruit

7. How are a poem and a juicy fruit alike?

_____

_____

    Poetry: Grade 4, SV 9894-9

Explore More

Classifying

Think about how words and things you read are alike. It can help you better understand what you are reading.

Read each group of words. Cross out the word that does not belong. Then write a category name for the words that are similar.

1. polite   helpful   manners   rude

   Category: _____

2. lick   bite   view   taste

   Category: _____

3. stem   bird   leaves   roots

   Category: _____

4. bowl   knife   fork   spoon

   Category: _____

5. skin   seed   rind   peel

   Category: _____

6. drink   throw   toss   pitch

   Category: _____

7. apple   orange   plum   carrot

   Category: _____

8. fingers   ring   legs   eyes

   Category: _____

LESSON 4

Elf and Dormouse

Poetry Skill: Alliteration

Standard
Identify words that develop auditory skills, including alliteration, onomatopoeia, assonance, and consonance

Explore Alliteration
Explain that alliteration is a sound device in which the beginning sound or sounds in two or more words are repeated. Have students tell what sound is repeated in *tugged till the toadstool toppled in two.* Challenge them to find other examples of alliteration.

Vocabulary

gaily–happily
heap–pile
lamented–cried out sadly
lest–worried
toadstool–mushroom
toppled–caused to fall
trembled–shook with fright
wee–tiny

Summary

This humorous poem explains how an elf invents the first umbrella.

Read the Poem

Introduce the Poem
Lead students in a discussion of how different inventions they know about were created. Then ask them to listen to a poem that tells how one item was invented.

Introduce the Vocabulary
Have students work in groups. Distribute copies of the word card on page 9. Encourage students to work together to complete a card for each word and discuss their findings. Gather the students and ask different groups to discuss a word you name.

During Reading

Invite volunteers to read the poem.

After Reading

Questions
1. What problems did the elf have? (*He wanted to get home, but it was raining, and there was a dormouse under the same toadstool.*)
2. How did the elf's feeling change during the poem? (*First, he was scared when he saw the dormouse. Then, he became happy because he found a way to stay dry and get home.*)
3. How is a toadstool like an umbrella? (*The toadstool has a long stem for a handle and its top is shaped like the canopy of an umbrella.*)

Fluency
Point out the exclamation point and the question mark in the poem. Model how the voice inflects differently for each. Have students rehearse the two sentences to develop fluency.

Develop Oral Language
Have students sit in a circle and explain that they will read the poem. Have one student read the first line. The person to the left (or right) reads the second line without pausing after the first reader. The reading continues with a new person reading each line. Challenge students to read the poem without changing rhythm or speed.

Writing

Ask students to write a humorous short story or poem of their own telling how another item was invented.

Lesson 4 • Elf and Dormouse: Teacher Information
Poetry: Grade 4, SV 9894-9

Name _____   Date _____

Elf and Dormouse
by Oliver Herford

UNDER a toadstool crept a wee Elf,
Out of the rain to shelter himself.
Under the toadstool, sound asleep,
Sat a big Dormouse all in a heap.
Trembled the wee Elf, frightened and yet
Fearing to fly away lest he get wet.
To the next shelter—maybe a mile!
Sudden the wee Elf smiled a wee smile.
Tugged till the toadstool toppled in two.
Holding it over him, gaily he flew.
Soon he was safe home, dry as could be.
Soon woke the Dormouse—"Good gracious me!
"Where is my toadstool?" loud he lamented.
—And that's how umbrellas first were invented.

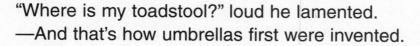

Elf and Dormouse: Assessment

Think about the poem. Then answer the questions. Fill in the circle next to the correct answer.

1. The elf flew under the toadstool to
   Ⓐ talk to the dormouse.
   Ⓑ go home.
   Ⓒ get out of the rain.
   Ⓓ go to sleep.

2. After the elf broke off the toadstool,
   Ⓐ the dormouse woke up.
   Ⓑ he flew away.
   Ⓒ the rain stopped.
   Ⓓ he got scared.

3. When the dormouse "lamented," he probably was
   Ⓐ sad.
   Ⓑ happy.
   Ⓒ scared.
   Ⓓ lonely.

4. Another good title for the poem would be
   Ⓐ "Rain, Rain, Go Away."
   Ⓑ "The Sleeping Dormouse."
   Ⓒ "The Happy Elf."
   Ⓓ "Inventing the Umbrella."

5. The dormouse woke up because
   Ⓐ the elf woke him.
   Ⓑ he was getting wet.
   Ⓒ the toadstool fell on him.
   Ⓓ it was time to go home.

6. Why was the elf frightened?
   Ⓐ He was scared of flying.
   Ⓑ He was too far from home.
   Ⓒ The thunder was too loud.
   Ⓓ He was afraid of the dormouse.

7. How did the elf feel when he found a way to get home? Explain.

_____

_____

Synonyms

A synonym is a word that means the same or almost the same as another word.

Examples: start—begin   happy—glad

Read each sentence. Find a word in the box that means the same or almost the same as the word or words in dark print. Write the word on the line.

frightened	gaily	heap	lamented
trembled	toadstool	wee	toppled

1. Wanda raked the leaves into a **pile**.   _____

2. She stopped when she saw a **mushroom**.   _____

3. She remembered all the stories her
   grandmother used to tell her about **tiny** elves.   _____

4. "Some people were **scared** of them,"
   Grandma had said.   _____

5. "They **shook** with fear when an elf was
   around," she said.   _____

6. Grandma continued, "The elves **caused** the
   books **to fall** off of shelves for a trick!"   _____

7. "Then they would laugh **happily**," she said.   _____

8. Wanda **cried out sadly** that there were no
   elves to talk to today.   _____

Disguise

Summary

In this limerick, a dog looks vicious from the front, but his wagging tail dispels the mean image.

Read the Poem

Introduce the Poem
Lead students in a discussion of how they should act around dogs they do not know. Then ask students how they would act if they met the dog in the poem.

Introduce the Vocabulary
Write the words on the board and discuss their meanings. Have students fold a sheet of paper into quarters. Ask them to draw a picture to show the meaning of each word and to write a sentence using the vocabulary word to label the picture.

During Reading

Invite volunteers to read the limerick.

After Reading

Activity
Distribute the word wheel on page 10 to students and have them write all the words from the poem that describe the dog.

Fluency
Remind students that a limerick has a specific rhythm. Then model how to read a limerick. Invite partners to practice reading rhythmically.

Develop Oral Language
Invite partners to read the poem according to the rhyming words. One person reads the lines that have the rhyming "a" pattern, and the partner reads the lines with the "b" pattern. Then have partners switch lines.

Writing

Have students choose a favorite pet or animal and write describing words on a word wheel. Challenge them to write a limerick about their pet. Tell them that some words can be made up, like *waggy* in "Disguise."

Read the Poem

Disguise
by Anonymous

There once was a lady called Maggie,
Whose dog was enormous and shaggy,
The front end of him
Looked vicious and grim
But the back end was friendly and waggy.

Lesson 5 • Disguise: Poem
Poetry: Grade 4, SV 9894-9

Disguise: Assessment

Think about the poem. Then answer the questions. Fill in the circle next to the correct answer.

1. Who owned the dog?
Ⓐ a man
Ⓑ a girl
Ⓒ a boy
Ⓓ a lady

2. While the dog wagged its tail,
Ⓐ it barked.
Ⓑ it looked grim.
Ⓒ it ate dinner.
Ⓓ it played with a ball.

3. A dog that is "shaggy" has
Ⓐ a big nose.
Ⓑ short legs.
Ⓒ a fat tummy.
Ⓓ long fur.

4. This poem is mostly about
Ⓐ a person who liked dogs.
Ⓑ large dogs.
Ⓒ a big, shaggy dog.
Ⓓ a dog that liked people.

5. Why did the poet title the poem "Disguise"?
Ⓐ The dog did not want to be seen.
Ⓑ The dog wore costumes.
Ⓒ The dog's looks did not match its actions.
Ⓓ A person dressed like a dog.

6. The dog probably
Ⓐ wanted to go for a walk.
Ⓑ was nice.
Ⓒ would bite.
Ⓓ wanted to be brushed.

7. If you saw this dog and owner in the park, would you be scared of the dog? Why or why not?

_____

_____

Antonyms

Explore More

Antonyms are words with opposite meanings.
    Examples: big—small   long—short   up—down

Read each sentence. Find a word in the box that means the opposite of the word in dark print. Write the word on the line.

enormous	front	grim	laughed
night	shaggy	under	vicious

1. Thomas has a **short-haired** dog. _____

2. The dog is **tiny**. _____

3. It sleeps **over** Thomas's bed. _____

4. One **day**, Thomas heard a tapping noise. _____

5. The dog growled in a **friendly** way. _____

6. The dog's face looked **kind**. _____

7. It looked out the **back** window. _____

8. Thomas **cried** because a tree branch blowing against the window was making the scary noise. _____

Lesson 5 • Disguise: Vocabulary Skills
Poetry: Grade 4, SV 9894-9

[from] The Elephant's Child

Summary

Rudyard Kipling discusses the differences between adult questions and those of children in this excerpt from his famous story.

Read the Poem

Introduce the Poem

Open the discussion by telling students about a question that you have wondered about. Then invite students to share their interesting questions. Point out that questions begin with *who, what, where, when, how,* and *why.* Then ask students to complete the KWHL chart on page 12 to focus on a question they have. Have them complete the *K, W,* and *H* columns. Then as students read the poem, have them complete the last column in the chart. Finally, have students who know the story of *The Elephant's Child* share it.

Introduce the Vocabulary

Write sentences on the board using the vocabulary words. Underline the vocabulary words. Read the sentences and challenge students to guess the definitions of the vocabulary words. Discuss each answer, explaining how context can show if the guess is correct. After each definition is learned, have students suggest other sentences using the word.

During Reading

Read the poem out loud to students.

After Reading

Questions

1. Why does the poet let the serving-men rest? (*Most likely answer: He is working from nine to five.*)
2. Why does the poet capitalize the question words in the poem? (*He thinks of them as people. The names of people begin with capitals.*)
3. Why do you think that the little girl's serving-men get no rest? (*Most likely answer: Small children usually ask lots of questions.*)

Fluency

Point out that many poems have a rhythm, or beat. Model how to read the poem rhythmically. Have students read the poem to develop fluency.

Develop Oral Language

Have students use their own words to explain the poem.

Writing

Challenge students to research the question they had in Introduce the Poem and complete the KWHL chart. Then have them write a poem about their question.

Poetry Skill: Rhyming Words

Standard
Identify rhyme

Explore Rhyming Words
Remind students that some poems use rhyming words. Then have students find the rhyming word pairs and circle them using matching crayon colors. Guide students to understand that the even numbered lines rhyme. Then have students choose one of the word pairs and write other rhyming words on the word wheel on page 10.

Vocabulary

abroad–outside someone's country
affairs–business actions
folk–people
honest–telling the truth
tea–a practice of drinking hot tea and eating a snack in the late afternoon
views–ideas

Research Base

"To appreciate poetry is to appreciate the art of language." (*Guiding Readers and Writers: Grades 3–6, p. 410*)

Name _____   Date _____

[from] The Elephant's Child
by Rudyard Kipling

I keep six honest serving-men
    (They taught me all I knew);
Their names are What and Why and When
    And How and Where and Who.
I send them over land and sea,
    I send them east and west;
But after they have worked for me,
    I give them all a rest.

I let them rest from nine till five,
    For I am busy then,
As well as breakfast, lunch, and tea,
    For they are hungry men.
But different folk have different views;
    I know a person small—
She keeps ten million serving-men,
    Who get no rest at all!

She sends 'em abroad on her own affairs,
    From the second she opens her eyes—
One million Hows, two million Wheres,
    And seven million Whys!

Understand the Poem

[from] The Elephant's Child: Assessment

Think about the poem. Then answer the questions. Fill in the circle next to the correct answer.

1. When does the poet let the serving-men rest?
   - Ⓐ all night
   - Ⓑ in the afternoon
   - Ⓒ from nine until five
   - Ⓓ never

2. The serving-men rest
   - Ⓐ before they go to work for the young person.
   - Ⓑ after they have worked for the poet.
   - Ⓒ while they are working.
   - Ⓓ on holidays.

3. The poem says, "different folk have different views." "Views" are
   - Ⓐ windows.
   - Ⓑ ideas.
   - Ⓒ feelings.
   - Ⓓ dreams.

4. The main idea of this poem is
   - Ⓐ young people never stop asking questions.
   - Ⓑ people should give their workers a rest.
   - Ⓒ no one should talk during meals.
   - Ⓓ workers need to eat.

5. The serving-men are
   - Ⓐ real people.
   - Ⓑ lazy men.
   - Ⓒ children.
   - Ⓓ questions.

6. You can tell that the small person the poet knows
   - Ⓐ is very quiet.
   - Ⓑ asks many questions.
   - Ⓒ is not curious.
   - Ⓓ never sleeps.

7. Why do you think that the little girl in the poem asks so many questions?

_____

_____

Dictionary Skills

Explore More

A dictionary tells how to say a word and what it means.

Look at the pronunciation key. Then circle the word that matches the pronunciation.

a	add	**i**	it	**o͝o**	took	**oi**	oil
ā	ace	**ī**	ice	**o͞o**	pool	**ou**	pout
â	care	**o**	odd	**u**	up	**ng**	ring
ä	palm	**ō**	open	**û**	burn	**th**	thin
e	end	**ô**	order	**yo͞o**	fuse	**th**	this
ē	equal					**zh**	vision

ə = { a in *above*   e in *sicken*   i in *possible*
      o in *melon*   u in *circus* }

1. (hwâr) hair   war   where

2. (biz´ē) bells   buys   busy

3. (īz) eyes   ice   ails

4. (a fär´) after   affair   afar

5. (mil´yən) miles   million   mailing

6. (sûr´vənts) services   servants   survives

7. (vyo͞ow) view   value   vow

8. (on´ist) hoist   hostess   honest

My Shadow

Poetry Skill: Personification

Standard
Recognize the use of personification

Explore Personification
Explain to students that personification is a device in which human actions and ideas are given to things. Then discuss the examples, *The morning sun lightly kissed the flower*, and *The flame's fingers wrapped around the dry wood.* Challenge students to find examples of personification in the poem.

Vocabulary

arrant–extreme
coward–someone who is not brave
dew–drops of water that form on cool surfaces
notion–an idea
ought–should
proper–normal
shame–something to be sorry for
shoots–grows

Teacher Tips

"My Shadow" was written in the 1800s, so the language will be unfamiliar to children. Take the time to introduce the concepts of *nursie* and *india rubber* as they relate to life long ago.

Summary

Robert Louis Stevenson describes the actions of his shadow in this poem.

Read the Poem

Introduce the Poem
Bring several flashlights to class. Turn off the lights and ask students to experiment with light and shadows. After ten minutes, turn on the lights and invite students to share their observations.

Introduce the Vocabulary
Write the vocabulary words on the board. Have partners alphabetize the words, find the definitions in a dictionary, and record the meanings, noting words that have more than one meaning.

During Reading

Invite volunteers to read the poem.

After Reading

Questions
1. Why isn't the shadow like a proper child? (*A child grows slowly, but the shadow can change quickly from very tall to very small.*)
2. What time of day is it if the shadow is small? How do you know? (*It is noon, because the sun must be overhead to make the shadow small; or there is no light, which means there will be no shadow.*)
3. What does the poet think about his shadow? How do you know? (*He does not like his shadow because he thinks it is a coward and it stays in bed.*)
4. How does this poem show personification? (*The shadow does things like jump, grow, and stay in bed.*)

Fluency
Lead students in a discussion of how the topic of the poem and the words the poet selected contribute to the nonsense mood of the poem. Then read the poem several ways: fast and excited, slow and melancholy, and calm and happy. Have students tell which speed and voice reflect the mood of the poem. Then have partners practice reading the poem expressively.

Develop Oral Language
Invite students to alternate reading couplets.

Writing

Invite students to write rhyming couplets that personify familiar objects.
For example:
The wind danced with the falling snow
Twirling it high and dipping it low.

Name _____   Date _____

My Shadow
by Robert Louis Stevenson

I have a little shadow that goes in and out with me,
And what can be the use of him is more than I can see.
He is very, very like me from the heels up to the head;
And I see him jump before me, when I jump into my bed.

The funniest thing about him is the way he likes to grow—
Not at all like proper children, which is always very slow;
For he sometimes shoots up taller like an india-rubber ball,
And he sometimes goes so little that there's none of him at all.

He hasn't got a notion of how children ought to play,
And can only make a fool of me in every sort of way.
He stays so close behind me, he's a coward you can see;
I'd think shame to stick to nursie as that shadow sticks to me!

One morning, very early, before the sun was up,
I rose and found the shining dew on every buttercup;
But my lazy little shadow, like an arrant sleepy-head,
Had stayed at home behind me and was fast asleep in bed.

Lesson 7 • My Shadow: Poem
Poetry: Grade 4, SV 9894-9

My Shadow: Assessment

Think about the poem. Then answer the questions. Fill in the circle next to the correct answer.

1. The shadow is just like
Ⓐ other children.
Ⓑ the child in the poem.
Ⓒ the child's nurse.
Ⓓ a grown-up.

2. When does the shadow go before the child?
Ⓐ when the child goes out to play
Ⓑ when the child sees other children
Ⓒ in the morning
Ⓓ when the child goes to bed

3. The shadow "hasn't got a notion of how children ought to play." A "notion" is
Ⓐ an idea.
Ⓑ a game.
Ⓒ a question.
Ⓓ a feeling.

4. This poem is mostly about
Ⓐ a child and his nurse.
Ⓑ a child and his shadow.
Ⓒ a child and his friends.
Ⓓ a child and his dreams.

5. The shadow was not with the child at the end of the poem because
Ⓐ the sun was not up yet.
Ⓑ the boy made it stay in bed.
Ⓒ the shadow was tired.
Ⓓ the shadow couldn't play.

6. The poet most likely wrote this poem
Ⓐ to describe how shadows are formed.
Ⓑ to explain why he has a shadow.
Ⓒ to entertain people.
Ⓓ to describe shadow shapes.

7. Where is the light in the room when the child jumps into bed? How do you know?

_____

_____

Name _____   Date _____

Homographs

Homographs are words that have the same spelling but different meanings. Use words in the sentence to help you choose the correct meaning of a word.

Example: watch
Meaning A: to look at
Meaning B: a tool that tells time

Read each sentence. What does the word in dark print mean? **Write the letter for the meaning of the word.**

notions
Meaning A: ideas
Meaning B: thread or trim used in sewing

_____ **1.** Mrs. West had **notions** of hosting a grand ball.

_____ **2.** She bought fabric, thread, buttons, and other **notions** for her dress.

shoots
Meaning A: grows
Meaning B: young plants

_____ **3.** The green **shoots** pushed through the soil.

_____ **4.** One plant **shoots** up faster than the rest.

shadow
Meaning A: a dark space caused when something blocks the light
Meaning B: to follow

_____ **5.** A parent will **shadow** a child on the playground to make sure the child stays safe.

_____ **6.** Since it was a rainy day, there was not a **shadow** on the playground.

Lesson 7 • My Shadow: Vocabulary Skills
Poetry: Grade 4, SV 9894-9

LESSON 8

Stopping by Woods on a Snowy Evening

Summary

A poet traveling by sleigh through the dark, snowy woods stops to admire their beauty.

Poetry Skill: Format

Standard
Distinguish between fiction, nonfiction, poetry, and plays

Explore Format
Display a story and lead students in a discussion of the format they see, including paragraph formation and sentence length. Then pass out the poem and discuss the lines, verses, rhythm, and rhyme. Have students compare and contrast the poem and story formats on the Venn diagram on page 13.

Vocabulary

downy–light and fluffy
harness–straps that join something to a work animal
mistake–something that is not done correctly
promises–words saying that something will or will not be done
queer–odd
snowy–having snow
sweep–movement
village–small town

Read the Poem

Introduce the Poem
Have students draw a picture of a place that made an impression on them because of its beauty. Have them write a brief paragraph describing the place. Encourage them to use lots of adjectives in their writing. Then ask them to listen to one poet's thoughts about a place he found beautiful.

Introduce the Vocabulary
Write each word on a sentence strip, leaving spaces between each letter. Cut the letters apart and put the words into envelopes. Write the definition on the envelope. Pass the envelopes out to groups and have students unscramble the letters to find the words. Challenge them to use the word in a sentence.

During Reading

Ask volunteers to read the poem.

After Reading

Questions
1. What kind of feeling does the poem give? (*Most likely answers: quiet, peaceful*)
2. Why doesn't the man who owns the woods see the poet? (*The farmhouse was too far away and it was dark.*)
3. Why do you think the poet wrote "Stopping by Woods on a Snowy Evening"? (*to describe a scene that he thought was beautiful*)

Fluency
Help students explore how to read poems with line breaks. Model how to read the poem rhythmically and without pause at the end of an unpunctuated line. Then have partners rehearse the second verse of the poem several times.

Develop Oral Language
Invite partners to read the poem, alternating verses.

Writing

Ask students to review their drawing and paragraph completed in Introduce the Poem. Invite them to write a poem about the place. Challenge them to use words that capture the mood.

Read the Poem

Stopping by Woods on a Snowy Evening

by Robert Frost

Whose woods these are I think I know.
His house is in the village, though;
He will not see me stopping here
To watch his woods fill up with snow.

My little horse must think it queer
To stop without a farmhouse near
Between the woods and frozen lake
The darkest evening of the year.

He gives his harness bells a shake
To ask if there is some mistake.
The only other sound's the sweep
Of easy wind and downy flake.

The woods are lovely, dark and deep.
But I have promises to keep,
And miles to go before I sleep,
And miles to go before I sleep.

www.harcourtschoolsupply.com
43
Lesson 8 • Stopping by Woods on a Snowy Evening: Poem
Poetry: Grade 4, SV 9894-9

Name _____   Date _____

Stopping by Woods on a Snowy Evening: Assessment

Think about the poem. Then answer the questions. Fill in the circle next to the correct answer.

1. The poet thinks the woods
   Ⓐ are frightening.
   Ⓑ belong to someone he knows.
   Ⓒ are too dark to enter.
   Ⓓ are boring.

2. After the poet stops to look in the woods,
   Ⓐ his horse shakes his harness.
   Ⓑ he meets the owner.
   Ⓒ he goes to a farmhouse.
   Ⓓ it begins to snow.

3. The poem says, "My little horse must think it queer." "Queer" means
   Ⓐ fun.
   Ⓑ odd.
   Ⓒ ate.
   Ⓓ deep.

4. This poem is mostly about
   Ⓐ how to ride a horse.
   Ⓑ staying out of woods that are not yours.
   Ⓒ wanting to go home.
   Ⓓ enjoying a peaceful scene.

5. You can tell that the poet and his horse
   Ⓐ do not often stop on their way.
   Ⓑ are lost.
   Ⓒ are going to the village.
   Ⓓ like the cold.

6. The poet seems to be
   Ⓐ excited.
   Ⓑ sad.
   Ⓒ tired.
   Ⓓ angry.

7. Why doesn't the poet stop for long? How do you know?

_____

_____

Word Puzzle

Read each sentence. Choose a word from the box that correctly completes each sentence. Write the word in the puzzle.

> downy   harness   mistake   promises   queer   snowy   sweep   village

Across

3. Tin rode to the _____ to shop at the store.

5. The cover on the bed was filled with soft, _____ feathers.

6. Most children like cold, _____ days because schools close.

7. Pam made a _____ in her addition problem, so the answer was wrong.

Down

1. Hansel and Gretel thought the gingerbread house looked tasty but _____.

2. Long ago, a farmer would _____ a horse so he could hook up a plow.

4. Marcus _____ his father that he will clean his room before he leaves.

6. The cold winds _____ through the trees, causing the leaves to fall.

[from] Mr. Nobody

Poetry Skill: Repetition

Standard
Recognize the use of repetition

Explore Repetition
Repetition is a sound device in which sounds, words, or phrases are repeated to emphasize a point. As students read the poem, ask them why the poet might repeat the phrase *by Mr. Nobody*.

Vocabulary

agree–to have the same opinion or feeling
break–to crack
mischief–a playful action that causes trouble
oiling–putting oil on
prithee–old-fashioned word used to express a wish or request
scatters–spreads to different places
squeaking–a noise that is high and loud
tears–pulls apart

Teacher Tips

Students may find some of the language and ideas in "Mr. Nobody" difficult to understand. Explain that the poem was written long ago. Discuss the ideas, such as ink being spilled because of the use of ink pots and quills, with students.

Summary

Mysterious things happen around the house, so the poet thinks that Mr. Nobody is to blame.

Read the Poem

Introduce the Poem

Invite students to talk about some of the mysterious things that happen around the house. Ask them if they or a sibling gets blamed for the problem. Then have students suggest names of the real culprit. Ask them to listen to a poem in which a poet has the perfect suggestion.

Introduce the Vocabulary

Write the vocabulary words on the board and ask volunteers to look them up in a dictionary. Have a volunteer read all the definitions. Explain that some words have multiple meanings and ask students to identify the words that are in this category. Then have students read the poem to discover which meaning the words have in it.

During Reading

Invite volunteers to read the poem.

After Reading

Questions

1. How old do you think the person talking in the poem is? Why? (*Most likely answer: A young person is talking because the things described would most likely happen because of the carelessness of a young person.*)
2. Why does the poet describe the man as quiet? (*No one ever hears him.*)
3. Do you think Mr. Nobody makes trouble to be hurtful? Why or why not? (*Most likely answer: No, because the damage does not really hurt anyone.*)
4. Who is Mr. Nobody? (*children*)

Fluency

Help students explore how to read poems with line breaks that do not have ending punctuation. Model how to read the line breaks smoothly and fluently. Then have students practice reading the poem fluently.

Develop Oral Language

Have students sit in a circle, and explain that they will be reading the poem in couplets, or two lines. Have one person read the first two lines and have the next person on the left read the next two lines. Invite everyone to join in on the last lines of each verse that reference Mr. Nobody. Challenge students to keep the continuous speed of the poem as they take turns reading.

Name _____   Date _____

[from] Mr. Nobody
by Anonymous

I know a funny little man,
As quiet as a mouse,
Who does the mischief that is done
In everybody's house!

There's no one ever sees his face,
And yet we all agree
That every plate we break was cracked
By Mr. Nobody.

'Tis he who always tears our books,
Who leaves the door ajar,
He pulls the buttons from our shirts,
And scatters pins afar;
That squeaking door will always squeak
For, prithee, don't you see,
We leave the oiling to be done
By Mr. Nobody.

The finger marks upon the door
By none of us are made;
We never leave the blinds unclosed,
To let the curtains fade;
The ink we never spill; the boots
That lying 'round you see
Are not our boots;
They all belong to Mr. Nobody!

Name _____ Date _____

[from] Mr. Nobody: Assessment

Think about the poem. Then answer the questions. Fill in the circle next to the correct answer.

1. Who has seen Mr. Nobody?
   - Ⓐ only children
   - Ⓑ no one
   - Ⓒ people who are very quiet
   - Ⓓ only adults

2. Mr. Nobody is blamed
   - Ⓐ after something happens.
   - Ⓑ before something happens.
   - Ⓒ while something is happening.
   - Ⓓ for everything good that happens.

3. The door is left ajar in the poem. "Ajar" probably means
   - Ⓐ alone.
   - Ⓑ open.
   - Ⓒ broken.
   - Ⓓ empty.

4. Another title for this poem could be
   - Ⓐ "The Broken Plate."
   - Ⓑ "The Squeaking Door."
   - Ⓒ "The Noisy Man."
   - Ⓓ "It Wasn't Me!"

5. The people in the poem blame Mr. Nobody because
   - Ⓐ he causes a lot of trouble.
   - Ⓑ he is not careful.
   - Ⓒ they do not want to get into trouble.
   - Ⓓ he lives with them.

6. Next time something goes wrong,
   - Ⓐ the person who is responsible will admit that he or she did it.
   - Ⓑ Mr. Nobody will be blamed.
   - Ⓒ Mr. Nobody will be asked to find another place to live.
   - Ⓓ Mr. Nobody will clean up.

7. Does Mr. Nobody live in your house? If so, how do you know he is there? If not, who does the mischief?

_____

_____

_____

Name _____ Date _____

Homographs

Homographs are words that have the same spelling but different meanings.
Use words in the sentence to help you choose the correct meaning of a word.

Example: bat
Meaning A: a kind of animal that flies
Meaning B: a toy that hits a ball

 Circle the word that will correctly complete both sentences.

1. If the plate falls on the floor, it will _____.
   The workers took a _____ for lunch.

   crack   walk   break

2. Mr. Rogers _____ an ad from the paper.
   Large _____ rolled down the baby's face when she cried.

   drops   tears   rips

3. The children left dirty finger _____ on the door.
   Our teacher _____ the book to show where she stopped reading.

   marks   prints   opens

4. Mrs. Moreno _____ for work at nine o'clock each morning.
   Autumn is the time in which _____ fall off the trees.

   nuts   calls   leaves

LESSON 10

To Any Reader

Poetry Skill: Rhyming Words

Standard
Identify rhyme

Explore Rhyming Words
The use of rhyming couplets will help students develop an understanding of rhyming words. Have students find the rhyming word pairs in this poem and circle them using matching crayon colors. Then have students choose one of the word pairs and brainstorm other words that rhyme with that pair.

Vocabulary

bent–determined
intent–concentrating
lingers–stays somewhere, not wanting to leave
lured–attracted someone by offering something pleasing
nor–and not

Teacher Tips

Robert Louis Stevenson wrote many poems about children. This poem came from a book that had many such poems.

Summary

The poet reflects on memories as he thinks about childhood.

Read the Poem

Introduce the Poem

Lead students in a discussion of how people who are very focused on a job or task act. Make sure students understand that the people are preoccupied and may not always hear or respond appropriately. Then ask students to listen to a poem to discover why the poet cannot call to the child in the poem.

Introduce the Vocabulary

Write the vocabulary words and the definitions on separate cards. Pass them out to students. Say sentences with the words and challenge students to stand if they have the words and definitions that match. Discuss each vocabulary word. Then have students identify the two vocabulary words that rhyme.

During Reading

Read the poem aloud to students.

After Reading

Questions

1. What does the poet mean by "windows of this book"? (*Possible answers: "Windows" could be pages of the book or the poems themselves.*)
2. Who is the child that is far, far away? (*one who lived a long time ago*)
3. What does the poet mean by "knocking on the window"? (*Possible answer: reading the poems*)
4. What does the poet mean when he talks about the "child of air that lingers in the garden"? (*He is talking about the memories of being a child.*)

Fluency

Explain to students that it is very important to watch for punctuation as they read so that they can understand the sentences. Model how to read the entire first sentence by pausing for commas and reading line breaks smoothly. Then invite partners to practice reading the poem.

Develop Oral Language

Have students explain the poem in their own words.

Writing

Remind students that Robert Louis Stevenson wrote many poems for and about children in the 1800s. Then have them name favorite poets that write for children today. Ask them to find a favorite poem from one of these poets and compare it on a Venn diagram on page 13 with this Stevenson poem.

To Any Reader
by Robert Louis Stevenson

As from the house your mother sees
You playing round the garden trees,
So you may see, if you will look
Through the windows of this book,
Another child, far, far away,
And in another garden, play.
But do not think you can at all,
By knocking on the window, call
That child to hear you. He intent
Is all on his play-business bent.
He does not hear, he will not look,
Nor yet be lured out of this book.
For, long ago, the truth to say,
He has grown up and gone away,
And it is but a child of air
That lingers in the garden there.

Understand the Poem

To Any Reader: Assessment

Think about the poem. Then answer the questions. Fill in the circle next to the correct answer.

1. The child in the poem is playing
   Ⓐ on a playground.
   Ⓑ in a garden.
   Ⓒ near the woods.
   Ⓓ in a house.

2. Since the time he was in the garden, the child has
   Ⓐ grown and gone away.
   Ⓑ gone inside the house.
   Ⓒ climbed into the tree.
   Ⓓ read a book.

3. The child is intent on his play. "Intent" probably means
   Ⓐ not paying attention.
   Ⓑ in a tent.
   Ⓒ concentrating.
   Ⓓ unhappy.

4. This poem is mostly about
   Ⓐ a boy in a poetry book.
   Ⓑ what happens to little boys.
   Ⓒ how children are alike.
   Ⓓ the importance of reading.

5. The boy cannot be called because
   Ⓐ he is not able to hear.
   Ⓑ the garden is too noisy.
   Ⓒ he is an imaginary child.
   Ⓓ he doesn't want to come.

6. This poem is called "To Any Reader." But the poet seems to think that
   Ⓐ people will think that the child in the poem is real.
   Ⓑ children will be reading the book.
   Ⓒ his book will never be read.
   Ⓓ gardeners will be reading this book.

7. Why can't the child in the poem hear if someone knocks?

_____

_____

Explore More

Definitions

Definitions are the meanings of words.

Example: garden–ground used for growing fruits, vegetables, and flowers

Read each sentence. The words in dark print are the definitions. Find a word in the box that means the same as the word or words in dark print. Write each sentence using the word.

| bent | garden | gorgeous | intent | lingers | lured | window |

1. Juan is **concentrating** on reading his book.

_____

2. He is **determined** on learning about fish.

_____

3. He **stays** on a page about sharks.

_____

4. Juan's sister knocks on the **opening with glass**.

_____

5. She is working out in the **ground used for growing flowers**.

_____

6. "You should be outside on such a **beautiful** day!" Juan's sister says.

_____

7. But Juan ignores her and will not be **led away** from his book.

_____

LESSON 11

Hummingbird

Poetry Skill: Format

Standard
Distinguish between fiction, nonfiction, poetry, and plays

Explore Format
Remind students that a poem can be a short and quick picture of a feeling or thought a poet wants to share. Then lead students in a discussion of how the structure of "Hummingbird" shows that it is a poem. Guide the discussion so that students understand that not all poems rhyme.

Vocabulary

fairies–make-believe tiny people who have wings
perch–a place for a bird to rest
raindrops–drops of rain
steady–showing no movement

Research Base

"Students who are immersed in the vibrant sounds of poetry will write better poetry themselves; what's more, they are more likely to develop a lifetime appreciation for poetry."
(*Guiding Readers and Writers: Grades 3–6, p. 419*)

Summary

The poet wonders how the tiny hummingbird can hold still while in the air.

Read the Poem

Introduce the Poem
Distribute the KWHL chart from page 12. Have students complete the *K*, *W*, and *H* columns focusing on the topic of hummingbirds. Ask students to listen to a poem about a person who has questions about hummingbirds. Later in the day, allow students class time to find the answers to their questions and to complete the last column in their charts.

Introduce the Vocabulary
Divide the class into small groups. Assign each group a vocabulary word. Have them write the word on a word wheel on page 10. Challenge them to write other words that link the word to other images, concepts, or ideas that are related.

During Reading

Read the poem aloud to students.

After Reading

Questions
1. Who is the poet speaking to in the poem? (*the hummingbird*)
2. Why does the poet think the bird is not real? (*Other birds cannot hold still when they fly.*)
3. What does the poet think about hummingbirds? How do you know? (*She thinks they are wonderful and special because she compares them to fairies and flowers, two other things that are wonderful and special to most people.*)

Fluency
Point out that there are a lot of questions in the poem. Have students practice reading the poem with the proper intonation.

Develop Oral Language
Challenge students to memorize a favorite part of the poem to share with the class.

Writing

Point out that the poet uses lots of adjectives to describe the hummingbird. Ask students to choose another animal and use the word wheel on page 10 to write adjectives about that animal. Then challenge them to write a poem that describes the way it looks and how it behaves.

Name _____ Date _____

Hummingbird
by Hilda Conkling

Why do you stand on the air
And no sun shining?
How can you hold yourself so still
On raindrops sliding?
They change and fall, they are not steady,
But you do not know they are gone.
Is there a silver wire
I cannot see?
Is the wind your perch?
Raindrops slide down your little shoulders...
They do not wet you:
I think you are not real
In your green feathers!
You are not a hummingbird at all
Standing on air above the garden!
I dreamed you the way I dream fairies,
Or the flower I saw yesterday!

Lesson 11 • **Hummingbird:** Poem
Poetry: Grade 4, SV 9894-9

Name Date

Understand the Poem

Hummingbird: Assessment

Think about the poem. Then answer the questions. Fill in the circle next to the correct answer.

1. Where is the hummingbird?
   - Ⓐ near the garden
   - Ⓑ in the woods
   - Ⓒ in the house
   - Ⓓ by a lake

2. What does the hummingbird do when the poet sees it?
   - Ⓐ flies away
   - Ⓑ stands still
   - Ⓒ sits on a flower
   - Ⓓ drinks from a flower

3. "Steady" means
   - Ⓐ not moving.
   - Ⓑ not strong.
   - Ⓒ not wet.
   - Ⓓ not seeing.

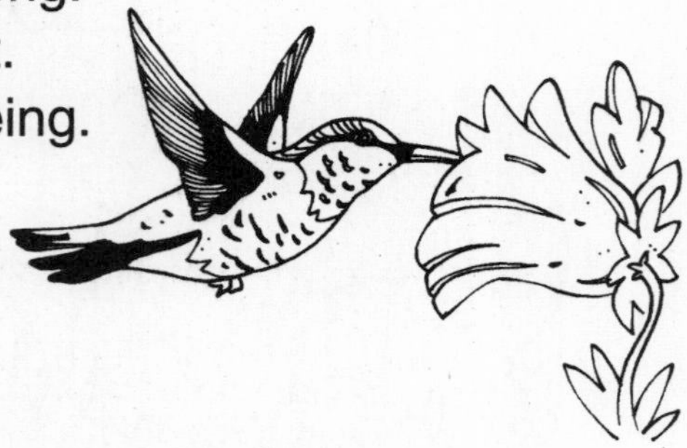

4. Another title for this poem could be
   - Ⓐ "My Garden."
   - Ⓑ "An Interesting Little Bird."
   - Ⓒ "My Pet Bird."
   - Ⓓ "Just a Dream."

5. Which word best describes the day?
   - Ⓐ sunny
   - Ⓑ windy
   - Ⓒ rainy
   - Ⓓ snowy

6. Why does the poet mention a silver wire?
   - Ⓐ She sees one near the bird.
   - Ⓑ She thinks the bird must be held up by one.
   - Ⓒ She put the wires in the garden herself.
   - Ⓓ She needs to buy one.

7. How do you know that "Hummingbird" is a poem?

Compounds

A compound word is a word made by putting together two or more smaller words.

Examples: outside   sidewalk

Draw a line to match one word in **Column A** with a word in **Column B**. Use each word only once. Write each new compound word in the box and draw a picture to show its meaning. On another sheet of paper, write a paragraph using at least three of the compound words.

Column A	**Column B**
1. rain	shine
2. humming	drops
3. sun	bird
4. thunder	storm

1.

2.

3.

4.

Lesson 11 • **Hummingbird:** Vocabulary Skills
Poetry: Grade 4, SV 9894-9

Voices of the Air

Poetry Skill: Personification

Standard
Recognize the use of personification

Explore Personification
Explain to students that personification is a device in which human actions and ideas are given to things. Then discuss the personification example in the second verse in which the sea and wind are given the human characteristic of sighing and making music with throats. Challenge students to find the other example in the fourth verse.

Vocabulary

basses–a very low musical sound
chord–three or more musical notes that sound pleasing together
droning–a steady, humming sound
ease–with little work
magical–having special powers
pod–a part of a plant that holds seeds
rare–not too often
shrill–having a sharp, high sound

Summary

The poet celebrates the special moments in nature when the small sounds of a bee or fly are louder and more noticed than the sea and wind.

Read the Poem

Introduce the Poem

If possible bring a conch shell to school and let students listen to the "ocean" as they hold it to their ear. Discuss the sounds that the ocean and wind make on the beach and how sometimes these sounds make it difficult to hear or talk to each other while at the beach. Then ask students to listen to a poem in which the poet talks about other sounds she hears.

Introduce the Vocabulary

Write sentences on the board using the vocabulary words. Read the sentences and challenge students to guess the definitions. Discuss each answer, explaining how context would show that the guess was correct. After each definition is learned, have students suggest other sentences using the word.

During Reading

Ask volunteers to read the poem.

After Reading

Questions

1. Where is the poet? How do you know? (*She is at the beach, because she talks about the sea.*)
2. What does the poet compare the sounds of nature to? (*music*)
3. What sounds does the poet hear? (*Accept onomatopoeic sounds, such as buzz, tap, pop and shh.*)
4. How does the poet feel about nature? (*She thinks it is magical and a surprise.*)

Fluency

Explain that expression is the way a poem is read. Then lead students in a discussion of the mood of the poem. Ask if the poet is excited or calm or happy or sad. Then read the poem several ways: fast and excited, slow and melancholy, and calm and happy. Have students tell which speed and voice reflect the mood of the poem. Point out how the words and images dictate the mood. Finally, have students practice reading the poem expressively.

Develop Oral Language

Have partners alternate reading the verses of the poem. Challenge them to pay attention to mood.

Read the Poem

Voices of the Air

by Katherine Mansfield

But then there comes that moment rare
When, for no cause that I can find,
The little voices of the air
Sound above all the sea and wind.

The sea and wind do then obey
And sighing, sighing, double notes
Of double basses, content to play
A droning chord for the little throats—

The little throats that sing and rise
Up into the light with lovely ease
And kind of magical, sweet surprise
To hear and know themselves for these—

For these little voices: the bee, the fly,
The leaf that taps, the pod that breaks,
The breeze on the grass-tops bending by,
The shrill, quick sound that the insect makes.

www.harcourtschoolsupply.com
59
Lesson 12 • Voices of the Air: Poem
Poetry: Grade 4, SV 9894-9

Name _____   Date _____

Voices of the Air: Assessment

✎ **Think about the poem. Then answer the questions. Fill in the circle next to the correct answer.**

1. Which is a "voice" in the poem that the poet hears?
   Ⓐ a child that cries
   Ⓑ a bird that chirps
   Ⓒ a horn that beeps
   Ⓓ a leaf that taps

2. What happens when the little voice begins to sound?
   Ⓐ The wind begins to blow.
   Ⓑ The waves crash on the sand.
   Ⓒ The wind and sea become background music.
   Ⓓ The pods spread seed.

3. Which of these is a "shrill" sound?
   Ⓐ a moo of a cow
   Ⓑ a drum
   Ⓒ a whistle
   Ⓓ a book closing

4. The poem is all about
   Ⓐ looking for small joys in life.
   Ⓑ going to the beach.
   Ⓒ singing songs and playing basses.
   Ⓓ insects that make noise.

5. The small voices are noticed most likely because
   Ⓐ they are louder at night.
   Ⓑ they are closer to the poet.
   Ⓒ they surprise the poet.
   Ⓓ the other noises are gone.

6. What can you tell about the poet?
   Ⓐ She lives at the beach.
   Ⓑ She spends time outside.
   Ⓒ She likes to sing.
   Ⓓ She gives singing lessons.

7. Does the poet like to hear the little voices? How do you know?

   _____

   _____

Antonyms

Antonyms are words with opposite meanings.
   Examples: big—small   long—short   up—down

 Read each sentence. Circle the words that are antonyms.

1. The little children looked at the big tiger.

2. Jason played on his computer after he worked on his math assignment.

3. The shrill flute sound broke into the droning violins.

4. The grass will bend and straighten as the wind blows.

5. Mira lost her mitten but found it in her coat pocket the next day.

6. After a while, sweet milk will sour.

7. The sun rises in the morning and sets in the evening.

8. It is common for Kim to look for rare birds when she hikes.

I Wandered Lonely as a Cloud

Summary

A field filled with daffodils lifts the mood of the poet on his walk and brings him joy during different times of the year when he is deep in thought.

Read the Poem

Introduce the Poem

Lead students in a discussion of how they feel when they are in a bad, lonely, or grumpy mood. Then invite them to share what they do to make themselves feel happier. Ask students to listen to how one poet deals with his bad mood.

Introduce the Vocabulary

Using the graph on page 11, make a word find puzzle. Write the words to be found at the bottom of the page. After students find the words in the puzzle, have them find the definitions in a dictionary and record the meanings on the puzzle.

During Reading

Read the poem aloud to students.

After Reading

Questions

1. How does the poet feel at the beginning of the poem? (*lonely*)
2. How many daffodils did the poet see? How do you know? (*He saw a field full; he compares them to the number of stars in the Milky Way.*)
3. Do you think the poet spends much time alone? Explain. (*Yes, he spends time alone because he was alone when he found the daffodils, and he talks about "the bliss of solitude."*)
4. How does the poet feel at the end of the poem? (*happy and joyous*)

Fluency

Explain to students that commas, colons, semicolons, and dashes signal that a reader should pause briefly. Then model reading the first verse of the poem, pausing appropriately at punctuation. Have students read the poem several times to develop fluency.

Develop Oral Language

Assign four students to each group and have them rehearse an oral presentation of the poem.

Writing

Invite students to write a paragraph or poem telling about something that lifts their spirits when they are in an unhappy mood.

Read the Poem

I Wandered Lonely as a Cloud
by William Wordsworth

I wandered lonely as a cloud
That floats on high over vales and hills,
When all at once I saw a crowd,
A host, of golden daffodils;
Beside the lake, beneath the trees,
Fluttering and dancing in the breeze.

Continuous as the stars that shine
And twinkle on the Milky Way,
They stretched in never-ending line
Along the margin of a bay:
Ten thousand saw I at a glance,
Tossing their heads in sprightly dance.

The waves beside them danced; but they
Out-did the sparkling waves in glee:
A poet could not but be gay,
In such jocund company:
I gazed—and gazed—but little thought
What wealth the show to me had brought:

For oft, when on my couch I lie
In vacant or in pensive mood,
They flash upon that inward eye
Which is the bliss of solitude;
And then my heart with pleasure fills,
And dances with the daffodils.

I Wandered Lonely as a Cloud: Assessment

Think about the poem. Then answer the questions. Fill in the circle next to the correct answer.

1. Where did the poet see the daffodils?
- Ⓐ by his couch
- Ⓑ in his garden
- Ⓒ by the lake
- Ⓓ along the road

2. After the poet thinks about the daffodils,
- Ⓐ his heart fills with pleasure.
- Ⓑ he gets lonely.
- Ⓒ he goes to look for the flowers.
- Ⓓ he dances.

3. Which words mean the same?
- Ⓐ wander, lonely
- Ⓑ gazed, thought
- Ⓒ vales, hills
- Ⓓ crowd, host

4. The poem is mostly about
- Ⓐ the Milky Way.
- Ⓑ hiking by the lake.
- Ⓒ the beauty of daffodils.
- Ⓓ being lonely.

5. The daffodils made the poet feel
- Ⓐ lonely.
- Ⓑ sleepy.
- Ⓒ sad.
- Ⓓ joyful.

6. What season is it in the poem?
- Ⓐ winter
- Ⓑ spring
- Ⓒ fall
- Ⓓ summer

7. What does the poet mean when he says that the daffodils were "tossing their heads in sprightly dance"?

_____

_____

Classifying

Explore More

Think about how words and things you read are alike. It can help you better understand what you are reading.

Read each group of words. Cross out the word that does not belong. Then write a category name for the words that are similar.

1. vales   canyons   lakes   valleys

Category: _____

2. child   crowd   host   group

Category: _____

3. glanced   heard   looked   gazed

Category: _____

4. glee   joy   angry   happy

Category: _____

5. carrot   daffodil   rose   petunia

Category: _____

6. twinkle   sparkle   shine   float

Category: _____

7. heart   eye   shoe   ear

Category: _____

8. poet   book   writer   author

Category: _____

The Face of the Mountain

Poetry Skill: Concrete Poem

Standard
Identify a concrete poem

Explore a Concrete Poem
Tell students that some poems are quick snapshots of an idea. Poets use words carefully to tell about a picture or feeling. Then tell students that some poets even make the words of a poem into shapes to give a better idea about the poem.

Vocabulary

endless–lasting or going on forever
etched–cut a picture or design in something, usually with acid
rocky–covered with rocks
snowy–covered with snow
timeless–having no end
trenches–long narrow ditches

Research Base

"**Poetry** is an essential, integral part of the language/literacy curriculum . . . ." (*Guiding Readers and Writers: Grades 3–6, p. 414*)

Summary

Using a concrete poem format and figurative language, the poet describes a mountain as an old person.

Read the Poem

Introduce the Poem
Have students look at the poem. Ask them what is different about this poem from other ones they have read. Lead students in a discussion of why a poet might make the words in a poem into a shape.

Introduce the Vocabulary
Write the vocabulary words and the definitions on the board. Lead students in a brief discussion of the words. Then have students create a word puzzle with the words using the graph on page 11. Challenge students to write sentences as clues to complete the puzzle.

During Reading

Ask a volunteer to read the poem.

After Reading

Activity
Remind students that a metaphor compares two things that are unlike. Metaphors do not use the words *like* or *as*. Then ask them what the mountain is being compared to. Have partners complete the Venn diagram on page 13 to show how the poet compares the mountain with an old person.

Fluency
Tell students that the three dots in a row is a kind of punctuation called ellipsis points. Tell students that when they see ellipsis points, they should briefly pause. Invite students to practice reading the poem fluently by pausing each time they see ellipsis points.

Develop Oral Language
Challenge students to extend the poem by thinking of more metaphors they could say to compare a mountain and an old person.

Writing

Invite students to choose another object and write a concrete poem about it.

The Face of the Mountain

by Margaret Fetty

The
morning
sun rises and
lightly touches
your snowy hair. It
then begins to shine
on your face, set in stone
and deeply etched with trenches.
Trying to reach the warmth, you lift
rocky fingers toward the sky. Timeless…
endless…you are a beautiful sight!

Name _____ Date _____

The Face of the Mountain: Assessment

Think about the poem. Then answer the questions. Fill in the circle next to the correct answer.

1. What does the mountain lift toward the sky?
   Ⓐ fingers
   Ⓑ hair
   Ⓒ face
   Ⓓ trenches

2. What does the sun shine on first?
   Ⓐ trenches
   Ⓑ face
   Ⓒ fingers
   Ⓓ hair

3. The poet says the mountain is "endless." What could she be talking about?
   Ⓐ the trails
   Ⓑ the number of rocks
   Ⓒ the view
   Ⓓ the snow

4. The poem
   Ⓐ describes a beautiful mountain.
   Ⓑ tells how to climb a mountain.
   Ⓒ gives facts about the sun.
   Ⓓ talks about an old man.

5. Where is the snow on the mountain?
   Ⓐ on the side
   Ⓑ on a trail
   Ⓒ on a peak
   Ⓓ in a trench

6. What time of day is it?
   Ⓐ afternoon
   Ⓑ night
   Ⓒ morning
   Ⓓ noon

7. How is this poem different from other poems?

_____

_____

Name _____   Date _____

Suffixes

A suffix is a small word part added to the end of a root word that changes the word's meaning.

Root Word	Suffix	Meaning	Example
hope	ful	full of	hopeful
end	less	without	endless
light	ly	in a certain way	lightly

Read each sentence. Underline each word that has a suffix. Tell the meaning of the word. Use a dictionary if you need to.

1. Tran was cheerful as he walked along the mountain trail.

   Meaning: _____

2. He walked quietly.

   Meaning: _____

3. He was hopeful that he would see some small animals.

   Meaning: _____

4. Suddenly, Tran stopped.

   Meaning: _____

5. A helpless baby bird hopped under a tree.

   Meaning: _____

6. Tran decided it would be careless to leave the bird, so he picked it up and took it to a park ranger.

   Meaning: _____

LESSON 15

The Tower and the Falcon

Poetry Skill: Personification

Standard
Recognize the use of personification

Explore Personification
Explain to students that personification is a device in which human actions and ideas are given to things. Then discuss the examples, *The flowers nodded their lovely heads* and *The grandfather clock stood at attention, guarding the entrance of the house.* Challenge students to find examples of personification in the poem.

Vocabulary

falcon–a bird that is a strong flyer
proudest–feeling best about something one does
tower–a tall, narrow building

Research Base

"**Poetry** is a microcosm for learning. Through the precise, concise language of poetry, students learn a lot about reading and writing." (*Guiding Readers and Writers: Grades 3–6, p. 421*)

Summary

A lonely tower in London, England, looks at himself differently with the help of a falcon.

Read the Poem

Introduce the Poem
Invite students to share times they feel lonely and what they do to make themselves feel better. Then invite them to listen to a poem about something that feels lonely.

Introduce the Vocabulary
Write the vocabulary words on the board and have partners find them in a dictionary. Challenge partners to write a sentence using each word. Then ask students to share their definitions and sentences.

During Reading

Read the poem aloud to students.

After Reading

Activity
Remind students that a poem can tell a story in the same way a book can. The poem can describe characters, have a setting, a problem, and events that lead to a solution. Draw a story map on the board and have students complete it after they read the poem.

Fluency
Point out the quotations marks and explain that they indicate that someone is talking. Discuss how a character would read those words. Have partners take turns reading the sentences as the falcon would say them.

Develop Oral Language
Assign students to groups and invite them to perform a dramatic reading of the poem.

Writing

Invite students to choose another kind of structure, such as a stone wall, house, or bridge, and to follow the wording and format of the poem to create a poem innovation.

Name _____ Date _____

The Tower and the Falcon
by Hilda Conkling

There was a tower, once,
In a London street.
It was the highest, widest, thickest tower,
The proudest, roundest, finest tower
Of all towers.
English men passed it by:
They could not see it all
Because it went above tree-tops and clouds.

It was lonely up there where the trees stopped
Until one day
A blue falcon came flying.
He cried:
"Tower! Do you know you are the highest, finest, roundest,
The tallest, proudest, greatest,
Of all the towers
In all the world?"

He went away.
That night the tower made a new song
About himself.

The Tower and the Falcon: Assessment

Think about the poem. Then answer the questions. Fill in the circle next to the correct answer.

1. Who spoke to the tower?
Ⓐ English men
Ⓑ a sparrow
Ⓒ a falcon
Ⓓ a cloud

2. Before the bird came by,
Ⓐ the tower felt lonely.
Ⓑ the tower felt grand.
Ⓒ the tower was tired.
Ⓓ the tower was singing.

3. The "English men" in the poem probably live in
Ⓐ Spain.
Ⓑ France.
Ⓒ England.
Ⓓ America.

4. This poem is mostly about
Ⓐ a foreign city.
Ⓑ life above the trees.
Ⓒ a blue falcon.
Ⓓ feeling lonely.

5. The people who pass by the tower probably
Ⓐ do not know that it is there.
Ⓑ do not think much of it because they are used to it.
Ⓒ speak to it each time they pass.
Ⓓ enjoy looking at it.

6. The "new song" that the tower made was most likely
Ⓐ a happier song.
Ⓑ a bird's song.
Ⓒ a lonely song.
Ⓓ a loud song.

7. When has a friend helped you sing a "new song"?

_____

_____

Name _____   Date _____

Words in Context

Use other words in sentences to help you find the missing word.

Read each sentence. Find a word
from the box to complete it. Then write the
word on the line.

claws	clouds	English	falcon
gloves	proudest	strongest	tower

1. The _____ is a kind of bird with pointed wings.

2. They are some of the _____ birds in nature because they can catch other animals while flying in the air.

3. It is a very strong flyer that can soar as high as the _____.

4. It was a popular hobby among the _____ people long ago to train the birds to hunt.

5. The owners wore heavy leather _____ on their hands and arms.

6. The owners needed to protect themselves from the sharp

   _____ on the birds' feet.

7. The _____ owners believed their birds were the best in all the land.

8. Some owners kept birds in a _____ of the castle and hired someone to care for them.

Basho's Haiku

Standard
Identify a haiku poem

Explore a Haiku Poem
Write one of the haiku poems on the board. Explain that a haiku is a kind of formula poem that originated in Japan. It focuses on one specific image that is supposed to set a mood or emotion. A haiku has three lines and a total of 17 syllables, often distributed in a specific 5–7–5 pattern. Help students count the syllables of the poem.

Vocabulary

creeps–moves slowly
delighted–given great pleasure
glinting–shining
harvest moon–the full moon at the time when crops are gathered
narrow–not wide
scythe–a tool that cuts like a knife
swath–a path cut through a field
violets–small purple flowers

Summary

Basho, a seventeenth-century Japanese poet, wrote many haiku, four of which focus on traveling.

Read the Poem

Introduce the Poem
In advance, research Matsuo Basho, a Japanese poet who mastered the art of the haiku. Share the information with the students. Then tell them they will read four examples of Basho's haiku.

Introduce the Vocabulary
Write the vocabulary words and the definitions on separate cards. Pin them to a bulletin board. Say a sentence with a vocabulary word and ask a volunteer to find the word and the definition that matches. Discuss the meanings.

During Reading

Ask volunteers to read the haiku.

After Reading

Activity
Ask students to choose one of the haiku and draw a picture to illustrate it. Challenge them to capture the mood of the poem as well as the image. Then pair students and have them use the Venn diagram on page 13 to compare their poems.

Fluency
Remind students that if there is no punctuation at the end of a line, they should continue reading without pause. Then ask students to fluently rehearse the poems.

Develop Oral Language
Challenge students to memorize one of the haiku and share it with the class.

Writing

Ask students to draw a picture of a favorite place they have visited. Invite them to write a haiku about it.

Read the Poem

Basho's Haiku
by Matsuo Basho

Haiku 1
Traveling this high
mountain trail, delighted
by the violets

Haiku 2
Through frozen rice fields,
moving slowly on horseback,
my shadow creeps by

Haiku 3
The bright harvest moon
keeps me walking all night long
around the little pond

Haiku 4
On high narrow road
old traveler clears wide swath,
tiny scythe glinting

75

Basho's Haiku: Assessment

Think about the poem. Then answer the questions. Fill in the circle next to the correct answer.

1. What did the poet walk around all night long?
   - Ⓐ a mountain
   - Ⓑ a pond
   - Ⓒ rice fields
   - Ⓓ horses

2. What happened before the poet saw the violets?
   - Ⓐ He rode a horse.
   - Ⓑ He walked around a pond.
   - Ⓒ He harvested rice.
   - Ⓓ He traveled on a mountain trail.

3. A scythe would cut
   - Ⓐ trees.
   - Ⓑ meat.
   - Ⓒ grasses.
   - Ⓓ ice.

4. These poems are mostly about
   - Ⓐ traveling.
   - Ⓑ riding horses.
   - Ⓒ looking at nature.
   - Ⓓ harvesting crops.

5. The poet moves slowly on horseback because
   - Ⓐ it is hot.
   - Ⓑ he doesn't want to slide on the ice.
   - Ⓒ the mountain is steep.
   - Ⓓ he is riding at night.

6. The poet walks around the pond at night because
   - Ⓐ the bright light keeps him awake.
   - Ⓑ he can see the violets.
   - Ⓒ that's when he harvests rice.
   - Ⓓ the road was finally cut wider.

7. Which is your favorite haiku? Why?

_____

_____

Name _____ Date _____

Explore More

Synonyms

A synonym is a word that means the same or almost the same as another word.

Examples: start—begin   happy—glad

Read each sentence. Find a word in the box that means the same or almost the same as the word or words in dark print. Write the word on the line.

delighted	field	large	narrow
scythe	swath	tiny	trail

1. Beth and her father were **very happy** to be hiking in the woods.

   _____

2. They walked along a **path** and talked.

   _____

3. Suddenly, the path became **very thin** because vines grew in it.

   _____

4. "I wish I had a **knife** to widen the path," Mr. Davis said.

   _____

5. "We could cut a **row through the plants** in no time," he said.

   _____

6. "Isn't that a **big** tool?" asked Beth.

   _____

7. "Some are very **small**," answered Mr. Davis.

   _____

8. "I think we should walk through the **meadow** so we do not trip on the vines," said Beth.

   _____

Lesson 16 • Basho's Haiku: Vocabulary Skills
Poetry: Grade 4, SV 9894-9

The Windmill

Standard
Identify rhyme

Explore Rhyming Words
Remind students that some poems use rhyming words. Then have students find the rhyming word pairs in the poem and circle them using matching crayon colors. Challenge students to find the rhyming pattern. Then have them choose one of the rhyming word pairs and write other rhyming words on the word wheel on page 10.

Vocabulary

devour–to eat
din–noise
flails–simple tools made of wood used to help separate seeds from the plant
fling–to throw carelessly
foe–enemy
granite–a kind of stone that is hard
melodious–musical
strive–to try hard
threshing–separating seeds from the plant
thrive–to be successful

Summary

A personified windmill talks about the job it does to bring success to the miller.

Read the Poem

Introduce the Poem

Help students make a pinwheel using plastic straws, straight pins, and construction paper. Once the pin is pushed through the "wheel" and the straw, bend the pin down with pliers and tape the point to the straw. Ask children how the pinwheel is like a windmill.

Introduce the Vocabulary

Write sentences on the board using the vocabulary words. Read the sentences and challenge students to guess the definitions. Discuss each answer, explaining how context would show that the guess was correct. After each definition is learned, have students suggest other sentences using the words.

During Reading

Invite volunteers to read the poem.

After Reading

Questions

1. What does the windmill in the poem do? (*grinds grain*)
2. What would make the windmill roar louder? (*The sails are turning faster because the wind is blowing harder.*)
3. What is personification? What are some examples of personification in the poem? (*Personification is a device in which human qualities and ideas are given to things. Accept all examples of personification.*)

Fluency

Explain that expression is the way a poem is read. Then lead students in a discussion of the kind of voice a "windmill character" might use to read the voice—big, booming, loud, confident. Invite students to practice reading the poem expressively.

Develop Oral Language

Remind students of the rhyming pattern. Then have partners choose either the "a" or "b" pattern. Challenge them to read the poem smoothly while reading only the lines of their rhyming pattern.

Writing

Have students imagine that the wind has heard the windmill talk and thinks it is the wind who should get the miller's thanks instead. Invite them to write a paragraph or poem from the viewpoint of the wind explaining why the wind is really the one to be thanked.

Name _____   Date _____

The Windmill
by Henry Wadsworth Longfellow

Behold! a giant am I!
　　Aloft here in my tower,
　　With my granite jaws I devour
The maize, and the wheat, and
　the rye,
　　And grind them into flour.

I look down over the farms;
　　In the fields of grain I see
　　The harvest that is to be,
And I fling to the air my arms,
　　For I know it is all for me.

I hear the sound of flails
　　Far off, from the threshing-floors
　　In barns, with their open doors,
And the wind, the wind in my sails,
　　Louder and louder roars.

I stand here in my place,
　　With my foot on the rock below,
　　And whichever way it may blow
I meet it face to face,
　　As a brave man meets his foe.

And while we wrestle and strive
　　My master, the miller, stands
　　And feeds me with his hands;
For he knows who makes him
　thrive,
　　Who makes him lord of lands.

On Sundays I take my rest;
　　Church-going bells begin
　　Their low, melodious din;
I cross my arms on my breast,
　　And all is peace within.

Name _____   Date _____

The Windmill: Assessment

Think about the poem. Then answer the questions. Fill in the circle next to the correct answer.

1. On which day does the windmill stop working?
- Ⓐ Monday
- Ⓑ Wednesday
- Ⓒ Sunday
- Ⓓ Tuesday

2. After its "granite jaws" devour the grains,
- Ⓐ the windmill rests.
- Ⓑ the windmill grinds them into flour.
- Ⓒ the miller feeds the windmill.
- Ⓓ the farmers thresh the grain.

3. "Devour" has the same meaning as
- Ⓐ destroy.
- Ⓑ eat.
- Ⓒ enjoy.
- Ⓓ foe.

4. This poem is mostly about
- Ⓐ a man who runs a windmill.
- Ⓑ a town and its windmill.
- Ⓒ what a windmill does.
- Ⓓ how farmers harvest grain.

5. The windmill is clearly
- Ⓐ the only one of its kind.
- Ⓑ very busy.
- Ⓒ unhappy with its job.
- Ⓓ afraid of the miller.

6. The miller most likely
- Ⓐ relies on the windmill.
- Ⓑ talks to the windmill.
- Ⓒ does not think about the windmill.
- Ⓓ repairs the windmill.

7. What are two clues that let you know the poem was written long ago?

_____

_____

80

Hink Pinks

Hink pinks are two words beside each other that rhyme. You can use hink pinks to solve riddles.

Example:
Riddle: What do you call the high area of land that a **mill** stands on?
Hink pink answer: A mill hill

Read each riddle. Answer it with a hink pink. (Hint: Think about the words in dark print.)

1. What do you call music made by **tin** instruments?

   A   __t__ __i__ __n__   ___ ___ ___

2. What do you call the **hour** that people eat?

   The   ___ ___ ___ ___ ___ ___

   __h__ __o__ __u__ __r__

3. What do you call the **miller** who feeds grain into the windmill?

   A   __m__ __i__ __l__ __l__ __e__ __r__

   ___ ___ ___ ___ ___ ___

4. What kind of enemy does a **crow** have?

   A   __c__ __r__ __o__ __w__   ___ ___ ___

LESSON 18

[from] Wynken, Blynken, and Nod

Summary

In this familiar lullaby, three fishermen sail in a wooden shoe to catch dreams.

Poetry Skill: Metaphor

Standard
Recognize the use of similes, metaphors, and personification

Explore Metaphors
Explain to students that a metaphor is a poetic device in which two things that are unlike are compared so that one is said to be another. Metaphors do not use the words *like* or *as*. Then discuss the examples, *The green grass was a carpet under our feet* and *The room was an oven.* Challenge students to find the examples of metaphors in the poem.

Vocabulary

crystal–something that is clear
dew–drops of water that form on cool surfaces
foam–bubbles in a group
folks–people
herring–a kind of fish
misty–having tiny drops of water in the air
trundle-bed–a low bed on wheels that is stored under a higher bed
wee–tiny

Read the Poem

Introduce the Poem
Lead students in a discussion of lullabies, their content, and their purpose. Then invite students to listen to an excerpt from the famous lullaby, "Wynken, Blynkyn, and Nod." Ask them to pay special attention to the kind of sounds that the poet uses.

Introduce the Vocabulary
Write the vocabulary words on the board. Have partners alphabetize the words, find the definitions in a dictionary, and record the meanings. Have students find the homophones, words that sound alike but have different spellings and meanings.

During Reading

Read the poem to students.

After Reading

Questions
1. How did the characters get the names they did? (*Possible answer: They were named for the eyes and head of a child who is falling asleep.*)
2. What is the "twinkling foam"? (*the stars in the sky; the Milky Way*)
3. What is the poet referring to when he says the characters "sailed on the beautiful sea"? (*They were sleeping.*)
4. The poet uses lots of words that have soft sounds, like /s/ and /sh/. Why do you think the poet did so? (*Since it is a lullaby, the soft sounds are pleasing for someone to hear.*)

Fluency
Lead students in a discussion of the mood of the poem. Point out that the way a poem is read, including speed and voice, should reflect the mood of the poem. Then read the poem several ways: fast and excited, slow and melancholy, and calm and paced. Have students tell which is the appropriate way to read the poem. Finally, have students practice reading the poem with the appropriate mood.

Writing

Challenge students to write and illustrate their own lullabies. Record the poems on a cassette or CD and share the lullabies with a parent or teacher who has young children.

[from] Wynken, Blynken, and Nod

by Eugene Field

Wynken, Blynken, and Nod one night
    Sailed off in a wooden shoe—
Sailed on a river of crystal light,
    Into a sea of dew.
"Where are you going, and what do you wish?"
    The old moon asked the three.
"We have come to fish for the herring fish
    That live in this beautiful sea;
    Nets of silver and gold have we!"
    Said Wynken, Blynken, and Nod.
All night long their nets they threw
    To the stars in the twinkling foam—
Then down from the skies came the wooden shoe,
    Bringing the fishermen home;
'Twas all so pretty a sail it seemed
    As if it could not be,
And some folks thought 'twas a dream they'd dreamed
    Of sailing that beautiful sea—
    But I shall name you the fishermen three:
        Wynken, Blynken, and Nod.
Wynken and Blynken are two little eyes,
    And Nod is a little head,
And the wooden shoe that sailed the skies
    Is a wee one's trundle-bed.
So shut your eyes while mother sings
    Of wonderful sights that be,
And you shall see the beautiful things
    As you rock in the misty sea,
    Where the old shoe rocked the fishermen three:
        Wynken, Blynken, and Nod.

Name _____   Date _____

[from] Wynken, Blynken, and Nod: Assessment

Think about the poem. Then answer the questions. Fill in the circle next to the correct answer.

1. Wynken, Blynken, and Nod sailed
   - Ⓐ in a boat.
   - Ⓑ on the moon.
   - Ⓒ in a wooden shoe.
   - Ⓓ in a tub.

2. After fishing all night,
   - Ⓐ the fishermen spoke to the moon.
   - Ⓑ they threw their nets to the stars.
   - Ⓒ they came down from the stars.
   - Ⓓ they went to sleep.

3. The fishermen sailed off "into a sea of dew." "Dew" is
   - Ⓐ salt water.
   - Ⓑ tiny drops of water.
   - Ⓒ a light rain.
   - Ⓓ snow.

4. Another title for this poem could be
   - Ⓐ "Fishing for Stars."
   - Ⓑ "Fishing with the Moon."
   - Ⓒ "The Little Lost Shoe."
   - Ⓓ "Shoe Tales."

5. Wynken, Blynken, and Nod are actually
   - Ⓐ great fishermen.
   - Ⓑ happy children.
   - Ⓒ the stars and the moon.
   - Ⓓ a child's eyes and head.

6. This poem was probably written
   - Ⓐ to tell about a bad dream.
   - Ⓑ as a lullaby for little children.
   - Ⓒ as a lesson for fishermen.
   - Ⓓ to teach someone to fish.

7. A metaphor is a way that poets compare two unlike things. What is the poet comparing when he says, "All night long their nets they threw/To the stars in the twinkling foam"?

_____

_____

Name _____   Date _____

Homophones

Some words sound alike, but they have different spellings and meanings.
Example: Sam used his **shoe** to **shoo** the bee away.
   shoe = something worn on the foot
   shoo = to scare away

Read each sentence. Circle the words that sound alike. Then find the words in a dictionary. Write the meaning of each word.

1. Mother and I went to see the sea.

_____

_____

2. We saw wee little crabs.

_____

_____

3. Do you know there can be dew on the sea grass early in the morning?

_____

_____

4. We stayed for two days, too.

_____

_____

LESSON 19

Mountain Brook

Summary

A poet describes a fast-moving mountain stream.

Read the Poem

Introduce the Poem
Have students who have seen a mountain stream or brook describe it using all five senses. Then ask them to listen to a poet's description of a mountain brook.

Introduce the Vocabulary
Using the graph on page 11, make a word find puzzle. Write the words to be found at the bottom of the page. After students find the words in the puzzle, have them find the definitions in a dictionary and record the meanings on the puzzle.

During Reading

Read the poem to students.

After Reading

Questions
1. Why do you think the poet compares the streamlet to lightning? (*Lightning is white and jagged in appearance. When a stream forms, melting snow trickles in jagged patterns, too, following the rocks.*)
2. What does the poet mean when she says the stream is "fresh as a flower"? (*Possible answer: She is comparing the new stream, which has just melted from snow or ice, to fresh water.*)
3. What are some other similes that you can think of to describe the streamlet? (*Answers will vary.*)

Fluency
Explain that many poems have a rhythm, or beat. Model how to read the poem rhythmically. Then invite partners to practice reading the poem with the same rhythm and speed.

Develop Oral Language
Have partners read the poem chorally.

Writing

Challenge students to write other similes to describe the stream as it continues down the mountain and flows into a lake.

Mountain Brook
by Elizabeth Coatsworth

Because of the steepness,
the streamlet runs white,
narrow and broken
as lightning by night.

Because of the rocks,
it leaps this way and that,
fresh as a flower,
quick as a cat.

Understand the Poem

Mountain Brook: Assessment

Think about the poem. Then answer the questions. Fill in the circle next to the correct answer.

1. What makes the water leap?
- Ⓐ fish
- Ⓑ cats
- Ⓒ flowers
- Ⓓ rocks

2. What does the poet compare the water to first?
- Ⓐ flowers
- Ⓑ cats
- Ⓒ lightning
- Ⓓ rocks

3. Which two words mean almost the same thing?
- Ⓐ leaps, stands
- Ⓑ quick, slow
- Ⓒ streamlet, brook
- Ⓓ narrow, rocky

4. The poem is mostly about
- Ⓐ a steep mountain.
- Ⓑ a small stream in the mountains.
- Ⓒ how cats move.
- Ⓓ lightning and rain.

5. When the poet sees the brook, she is probably
- Ⓐ at the bottom of the mountain.
- Ⓑ near the top of the mountain.
- Ⓒ in a desert.
- Ⓓ near a garden.

6. The water began as
- Ⓐ snow.
- Ⓑ lightning.
- Ⓒ flowers.
- Ⓓ rain.

7. How does the poet probably feel about the brook? How do you know?

_____

_____

Dictionary Skills

Explore More

A dictionary tells how to say a word and what it means.

Look at the pronunciation key. Then circle the word that matches the pronunciation.

a	add	i	it	o͝o	took	oi	oil
ā	ace	ī	ice	o͞o	pool	ou	pout
â	care	o	odd	u	up	ng	ring
ä	palm	ō	open	û	burn	th	thin
e	end	ô	order	yo͞o	fuse	th̶	this
ē	equal					zh	vision

ə = { a in *above*   e in *sicken*   i in *possible*
        o in *melon*   u in *circus* }

1. (lēps) lips   leaps   loops

2. (strēm) strum   stem   stream

3. (flou′ ûr) floor   flyer   flower

4. (nâr′ ō)
   narrow   narrator   nearer

5. (nīt) knit   neat   night

6. (līt′ ning) lighting   lightning   lighten

7. (moun′ tən)
   maintain   meadow   mountain

8. (bē cäz′) because   backs   beaks

Adventure

Poetry Skill: Format

Standard
Distinguish between fiction, nonfiction, poetry, and plays

Explore Format
Remind students that a poem is a short and quick picture of a feeling or thought a poet wants to share. Then lead students in a discussion of how the format shows that it is a poem. Guide the discussion so that students understand that not all poems rhyme.

Vocabulary

adventure–a new and exciting experience
hollow–a small valley
moaning–making a noise of pain or sadness
outline–a line that shows the outer shape of something
rest–to lie down
shadows–dark areas caused by something blocking the sun's rays

Summary

A poet is looking for adventure as she hikes.

Read the Poem

Introduce the Poem

Lead students in a discussion about a popular character in a movie, story, or computer game who gets to do lots of fun and exciting things in his or her adventures. Ask students what it would be like to be that character. Then invite them to listen to a poem about a poet who wants to have adventures.

Introduce the Vocabulary

Write the vocabulary words and the definitions on separate cards. Pin them to a bulletin board in any order. Then say a sentence with a vocabulary word and ask a volunteer to find the word and the definition that matches.

During Reading

Read the poem to students.

After Reading

Questions

1. How is the poet feeling in the poem? How do you know? (*Possible answers: She is lonely, bored, or frustrated. She is looking for something fun and exciting to do.*)
2. Where does the poet go to look for adventure? (*the woods, a hollow, and the shore*)
3. Do you think the poet would sail on a real trip if she could? (*Accept reasonable answers.*)

Fluency

Discuss with the students how the poet is feeling in the poem. Challenge them to read the poem with the expression that the poet feels.

Develop Oral Language

Assign students to work in groups and ask them to create a comic strip of the poem.

Writing

Point out to students that the poet did not use rhyming words. She simply wrote her thoughts to tell how she felt and what she saw one day. Invite students to write their own poem that tells about a thought or feeling. Encourage them to just write the ideas that pop into their heads.

Read the Poem

Adventure
by Hilda Conkling

I went slowly through the wood of shadows,
Thinking always I should meet someone:
There was no one.

I found a hollow
Sweet to rest in all night long:
I did not stay.

I came out beyond the trees
To the moaning sea.
Over the sea swam a cloud the outline of a ship:
What if that ship held my adventure
Under its sails?

Come quickly to me, come quickly,
I am waiting.
I am here on the sand;
Sail close!
I want to go over the waves . . .
The sand holds me back.
Oh adventure, if you belong to me,
Don't blow away down the sky!

Lesson 20 • Adventure: Poem
Poetry: Grade 4, SV 9894-9

Understand the Poem

Adventure: Assessment

✐ **Think about the poem. Then answer the questions. Fill in the circle next to the correct answer.**

1. Where does the poet look for adventure?
   Ⓐ in the city
   Ⓑ in the woods
   Ⓒ in a cave
   Ⓓ on a mountain

2. The poet sees the cloud
   Ⓐ after she comes out of the woods.
   Ⓑ after she sleeps in a hollow.
   Ⓒ after she walks on the sand.
   Ⓓ after she sees the boat.

3. In this poem, "outline" means
   Ⓐ weight.
   Ⓑ shape.
   Ⓒ size.
   Ⓓ drawing.

4. This poem is mostly about
   Ⓐ a girl taking a walk.
   Ⓑ a girl playing at the beach.
   Ⓒ a girl who is tired.
   Ⓓ a girl looking for adventure.

5. The girl does not stay in the woods because
   Ⓐ she does not find what she is looking for.
   Ⓑ the woods are frightening.
   Ⓒ she is looking for the beach.
   Ⓓ she is meeting someone.

6. What can you tell about the girl in the poem?
   Ⓐ She does not have any friends.
   Ⓑ She is tired of the things she usually does.
   Ⓒ She has sailed in many ships.
   Ⓓ She is ready to go back to school.

7. What kind of adventure would you like to have?

   _____

   _____

Explore More

Homographs

Homographs are words that have the same spelling but different meanings.
Use words in the sentence to help you choose the correct meaning of a word.

Example: ship
Meaning A: a large boat
Meaning B: to send or mail things

Read each sentence. What does the word in dark print mean? Write the letter for the meaning of the word.

hollow
Meaning A: a small valley
Meaning B: having a hole or empty space inside

_____ **1.** The bird builds its nest in a **hollow** tree.

_____ **2.** The Smiths built their house in the **hollow** on the other side of the mountain.

outline
Meaning A: a line that shows the outer shape of something
Meaning B: to draw the outer shape of something

_____ **3.** Manny will **outline** the picture in brown marker.

_____ **4.** His picture shows an **outline** of a ship.

rest
Meaning A: to lie down
Meaning B: something that is left

_____ **5.** Anna ate the **rest** of the cookies.

_____ **6.** Then she went to the bed to **rest**.

Poetry Grade 4 • Answer Key

Page 8
1. D
2. B
3. A
4. B
5. C
6. B
7. Answers will vary. Possible responses: It has short lines, and it rhymes. The poet talks about one idea.

Page 16
1. A
2. D
3. B
4. C
5. A
6. A
7. Possible answer: The poem has lines and verses, and the poem describes the changes of the moon in a quick, fun way.

Page 17
1. needs–must have kneads–mixes dough
2. knew–were familiar with new–not used
3. there's–there is theirs–belonging to them
4. by–in the direction of buy–to get something using money

Page 20
1. C
2. B
3. C
4. B
5. A
6. C
7. Answers will vary. Accept reasonable answers.

Page 21
1. squirming
2. bawl
3. approached
4. resembles
5. sturdy
6. grope
7. inclined
8. disputed

Page 24
1. B
2. A
3. A
4. B
5. D
6. D
7. Possible answer: They are both enjoyable.

Page 25
Categories may vary. Accept reasonable answers.
1. rude; kind character traits
2. view; things people do with food
3. bird; parts of a tree
4. bowl; tools people use to eat with
5. seed; the outer parts of fruits
6. drink; things to do with a ball
7. carrot; kinds of fruits
8. ring; body parts

Page 28
1. C
2. B
3. A
4. D
5. B
6. D
7. He was happy because he could stay dry and get away from the dormouse.

Page 29
1. heap
2. toadstool
3. wee
4. frightened
5. trembled
6. toppled
7. gaily
8. lamented

Page 32
1. D
2. B
3. D
4. C
5. C
6. B
7. Most likely answer: No, while the dog looks mean, his waggy tail means he is happy and friendly.

Page 33
1. shaggy
2. enormous
3. under
4. night
5. vicious or grim
6. grim or vicious
7. front
8. laughed

Page 36
1. C
2. B
3. B
4. A
5. D
6. B
7. Most likely answer: Young children ask questions because they are trying to learn.

Page 37
1. where
2. busy
3. eyes
4. affair
5. million
6. servants
7. view
8. honest

Poetry Grade 4 • Answer Key

Page 40
1. B
2. D
3. A
4. B
5. A
6. C
7. The light is behind the child because it would make the shadow in front of him.

Page 41
1. A
2. B
3. B
4. A
5. B
6. A

Page 44
1. B
2. A
3. B
4. D
5. C
6. B
7. The poet has someplace he needs to be. He says that he has promises to keep.

Page 45
Across
3. village
5. downy
6. snowy
7. mistake
Down
1. queer
2. harness
4. promises
6. sweep

Page 48
1. B
2. A
3. B
4. D
5. C
6. B
7. Answers will vary. Accept reasonable answers.

Page 49
1. break
2. tears
3. marks
4. leaves

Page 52
1. B
2. A
3. C
4. A
5. C
6. B
7. The child is a memory from the poet's childhood, so the child is not real.

Page 53
1. Juan is intent on reading his book.
2. He is bent on learning about fish.
3. He lingers on a page about sharks.
4. Juan's sister knocks on the window.
5. She is working out in the garden.
6. "You should be outside on such a gorgeous day!" Juan's sister says.
7. But Juan ignores her and will not be lured from his book.

Page 56
1. A
2. B
3. A
4. B
5. C
6. B
7. The poet focuses on just one idea and gives a glimpse into her thoughts about the idea. It also has short lines.

Page 57
Check that students draw appropriate pictures and write a paragraph using at least three of the words.
1. raindrops
2. hummingbird
3. sunshine
4. thunderstorm

Page 60
1. D
2. C
3. C
4. A
5. C
6. B
7. Yes, the poet likes to hear the voices because she calls them magical.

Page 61
1. little, big
2. played, worked
3. shrill, droning
4. bend, straighten
5. lost, found
6. sweet, sour
7. rises, sets
8. common, rare

Page 64
1. C
2. A
3. D
4. C
5. D
6. B
7. The wind was making the daffodils move as if they were dancing.

Page 65
Categories may vary slightly. Accept reasonable answers.
1. lakes; low landforms
2. child; things with people
3. heard; ways to look
4. angry; good feelings
5. carrot; kinds of flowers
6. float; ways that light moves
7. shoe; parts of the body
8. book; people who write

Poetry Grade 4 • Answer Key

Page 68
1. A
2. D
3. C
4. A
5. C
6. C
7. Possible answers: The poem is about a mountain, so the words form a mountain shape. Also, the poet describes the mountain as an old person.

Page 69
1. cheerful–full of happiness
2. quietly–in a quiet way
3. hopeful–full of hope
4. suddenly–in a sudden way
5. helpless–not able to take care of oneself
6. careless–not having care

Page 72
1. C
2. A
3. C
4. D
5. B
6. A
7. Answers will vary.

Page 73
1. falcon
2. strongest
3. clouds
4. English
5. gloves
6. claws
7. proudest
8. tower

Page 76
1. B
2. D
3. C
4. A
5. B
6. A
7. Answers will vary.

Page 77
1. delighted
2. trail
3. narrow
4. scythe
5. swath
6. large
7. tiny
8. field

Page 80
1. C
2. B
3. B
4. C
5. B
6. A
7. Most likely answers: Windmills were used long ago to make flour. Farmers were separating the seed from the plant with tools called flails.

Page 81
1. A tin din
2. The devour hour
3. A miller filler
4. A crow foe

Page 84
1. C
2. C
3. B
4. A
5. D
6. B
7. Answers may vary: fishing in the sea.

Page 85
1. see–to look at
sea–ocean
2. We–I and the other people in the group
wee–tiny
3. do–a question word
dew–drops of water that form on cool surfaces
4. to–too
two–the number 2

Page 88
1. D
2. C
3. C
4. B
5. B
6. A
7. She likes the brook, because she describes it by comparing it to things that people like.

Page 89
1. leaps
2. stream
3. flower
4. narrow
5. night
6. lightning
7. mountain
8. because

Page 92
1. B
2. A
3. B
4. D
5. A
6. B
7. Answers will vary.

Page 93
1. B
2. A
3. B
4. A
5. B
6. A

Reference
Fountas, Irene C. and Pinnell, Gay Su. 2001. *Guiding Readers and Writers: Grades 3–6.* Portsmouth, NH: Heinemann.